RESOLVING DISPUTES IN A GLOBAL ECONOMY

How to Resolve Conflict on a Global Basis including
Home, Work, and Community

Hezekiah Brown, PhD

The Reading Glass Books
1-888-420-3050
www.readingglassbooks.com
fulfillment@readingglassbooks.com

Table of Contents

About the Author

Hezekiah Brown
Arbitrator-Mediator

In 2003, Hezekiah Brown retired from his position as Deputy County Executive of Nassau County and moved to Elizabeth City, North Carolina.

He served as a member of the Board of Visitors at Elizabeth City State University, Member of the Elizabeth City-Pasquotank County Community Relations Commission and served on the Pasquotank County Planning Board.

He is a Veteran Arbitrator and Mediator who has developed his skills in the Corporate and Labor Relations field for more than 50 years. He is currently one of the foremost authorities in this profession. His expertise is regularly being sought by top Administrators on the State and National level as well as academia.

He is the former Director of Labor-Management programs at Cornell University where he taught arbitration, mediation, collective bargaining, contract administration managing conflict, anger management, problem solving, team building, change management, diversity. In addition, he wrote the curriculum for Cornell University Extension Dispute Resolution Certificate Program which attracted students from such counties as Saudi Arabia, Cypress, Italy, Bangladesh, South America, and Australia.

Hezekiah's other expertise is in conflict resolution, employment discrimination and joint labor-management training. He has worked in the Industrial and Labor Relations field for over 50 years serving as a negotiator for labor and management and served for 12 years as a Federal Mediator. In addition, he served as the Chief Mediator and Chairman of the New York State Mediation Board and a member of the Mario Cuomo Cabinet.

Hezekiah has mediated and arbitrated over 5000 Labor-Management and Community disputes in the United States including the Virgin Islands and Puerto Rico.

In 1992, he was selected as one of the ten instructors to visit Russia to teach Contract Administration and conflict resolution as they embarked on making the transition to the market economy.

In 1995, he was again selected as one of ten instructors to travel to Europe to study the Global application of Cooperation between Labor and management. Upon his return from Europe, he was selected by United States Secretary of Labor, Robert Reich to serve on the Labor-Management Task Force for excellence in State and Local Government. The recommendations were unanimously accepted by the United States Congress.

He has received numerous awards and recognitions for his work as a professional and Community Leader.

- Presidential Recognition Award for Community Service awarded by President Ronald Reagan
- The Federal Mediation and Conciliation Service Director's Award
- Black Achiever in Industry
- Martin Luther King Humanitarian
- Queens College Public Servant of the Year
- NAACP Community Service and Education
- Hofstra University Unispan Award
- Links Incorporated: Award of Appreciation Outstanding Public Service and Professional Achievement
- Hezekiah has been recognized by the Key Women of America; The Suffolk County Black Bar Association' The University of Bridgeport; National Association of Black School Educators; The Incorporated Village of Hempstead; The Tow of Hempstead; Nassau County and the State of New York.

In 1999, Hezekiah was elected to the Board of Trustees for the Incorporated Village of Hempstead, New York and ran for Mayor in 2001. He served on the Hempstead Board of Education.

In May of 2008, he was inducted into the Prestigious National Academy of Arbitrators.

Hezekiah received a Bachelor of Science Degree from State University of New York, Empire State College and was awarded an Honorary PhD. From Cornell University Extension.

Mr. Brown continued his community service in Elizabeth City, North Carolina and was awarded the AAPR Legend of the Year Award, Links Incorporated Public Service and Professional Achievement award, Lenora Jarvis-Mackey Award for Outstanding Commitment to Excellence in the community.

He served on the Elizabeth City/Pasquotank County Community Relations Commission, Vice-President of the Local Chapter of AARP, member of the Pasquotank County Planning Board, and Chairman of the Hope Group and serves as Chairman of the 20/20 Vision Committee, Celebration Our Diversity. Hezekiah served as a volunteer with the River City Youth Program.

He has been married to Chris Brown for 63 years and they are the proud parents of Rodney and Chandra, and one granddaughter, Crystal.

Hezekiah is an active member of Mt. Lebanon AME Zion Church.

In 1957, while serving as a US Army Paratrooper in the 101st Airborne Division (327 Airborne Battle Group), the Specialist Brown deployed to Little Rock, Arkansas to help enforce the desegregation of Little Rock Central High School.

- He who has a sharp tongue will soon cut his own throat.

- The right angle for approaching a difficult problem is the "Try angle."

- In every success story, you find someone has made a courageous decision.

- No one learns to make right decisions without being free to make wrong ones.

- Hate and anger are powerless when met with kindness.

- Be kind to unkind people –they need it the most.

- Kindness pays the most when you don't do it for pay.

- If you mind can conceive it, and your heart can believe it then you can achieve it.

- The thing to try when all else fails is again. Giving it another try is better than an alibi.

- Don't find fault, find a remedy.

- People forget how fast you did a job –but they remember how well you did it.

- If you speak when you are angry, you will make the best speech you will ever regret.

- Anger makes your mouth work faster than your mind.

- The love we give away is the only love we keep.

- Love is not only something you feel, it is something you do.

- Truth is not always popular, but it is always right.

- Where there is no vision people perish.

- When you see someone without a smile give them one of yours.

- All the roads to success is uphill.

- Success is getting up one more time than you fall.

- Teach us to make the most out of our time so that we may grow in wisdom.

- Love is seeking to make another person happy.

- When love and skill work together, expect a masterpiece.

- It takes courage to stand up and speak as well as it is to sit and listen.

- One of the best ways to persuade others is by listening to them.

- Proud people are always letting off esteem.

- No one ever injured their eye sight by looking on the bright side of things.

Look what happens when preparation meets opportunity.

MARQUIS
Who's Who®

Since 1898

Hezekiah Brown featured in
Who's Who in American in 2023!

Celebrating 50 years as a professional neutral, Arbitrator,
Mediator, Educator, Entrepreneur and Author.

Hez has resolved over five thousand labor-management, and community disputes and traveled to Russia, Europe, the Virgin Islands and successfully resolved disputes at the United Nations.

As a result of his outstanding professional career, he will be listed in Marquis Who's Who in America in 2023.

Confirmation Letter:

Dear Hezekiah Brown,

Congratulations on your inclusion as a Marquis Who's Who biographical listee! In order top recognize your distinction appropriately, we will feature you in our flagship hardcover registry, Who's Who in America.

Marquis Who's Who has been the world's preeminent biographer since 1899. Each year we strive to continue the tradition established by our founder, Albert Nelson, Marquis, over 120 years ago with the first publication of Who's Who in America. That mission is to profile those individuals who have made a difference by virtue of the positions of responsibility they hold and/or due to noteworthy accomplishments they have made.

I would like to congratulate you on the accomplishments that have captured the attention of the Marquis Who's Who Selection Committee. We are honored to recognize you among others in your specialized field and within the Marquis Who's Who organization and wish you all the best in your future endeavors.

Sincerely,
The Marquis Who's Who Editorial Team

Resolving Conflict Isn't Easy

We're all different. We look different. We believe in different things. We respond differently to situations. We want different results. Therefore, while our differences are things that make us unique when we're faced with opposing ideas, beliefs and structures, our differences cause conflict. Sometimes these conflicts create intense verbal debates; one side is arguing to prove that their ideas are better than the other side. And sometimes these conflicts cause such rifts that neither side wins and the matter goes unresolved. Conflicts have a strange way of allowing people to voice their opposing opinions and discover a way to compromise. Conflicts also have a strange way of creating so much animosity and tension. It seems easier to walk away with your beliefs intact instead of jeopardizing everything else.

I've spent years listening to people come together to argue their sides and draw up a resolution. My professions, and what I've come to recognize as my God-given talent is dispute resolution and negotiation. I have made a living from teaching people how to sit down, reluctantly sometimes, and voice their version of the story while also listening to the other party's version of the story. In some cases, both parties have realized that their disputes are frivolous or have no foundation to stand on. And in some cases, there's no denying that there's a serious issue at hand that absolutely must be resolved---and soon.

While I'd like to think of myself as a peacemaker, that's far from the technical skill and knowledge that is necessary to solve a dispute or negotiate a balanced resolution. It takes a special skill for listening, speaking, thinking, and investigating to perform the job that I hold near and dear to my heart. You would probably like to think that most people should naturally have the skill for listening, speaking, thinking, and investigating. After all, we are born with two ears, a mouth, and a brain and that is half of the battle. However, in times of dispute and conflict, while we are born with the right tools (ears, a mouth and brain), most people don't always use them, and they certainly don't use them properly.

Think about it: The last time you were in a conflict, where your opinions, beliefs and ideas opposed another person's, did you take the time to effectively listen to them, rebut with facts and findings, think before you speak, or otherwise approach the situation willing to compromise? If you did, then you are an impeccable communicator who can diffuse situations before they have a chance to develop. However, if you are one of the many who are headstrong on their opinion and really wants to "win" in a dispute, then in most cases, you have probably voluntarily avoided listening, speaking, thinking, and investigating. After all, who has time for all that when the main focus is to WIN!

What do I know about solving problems?

My profession has taken me to multiple countries, and I have worked in multiple industries. Whether it was education, politics, government or labor relations, there was always a dispute. The blue-collar employees would want something better than what the white-collar employees were offering. One political party blamed the other for the grievances of a city, state, or region. Teachers wanted something different than the administrators were willing to give. No matter what, the issue was always a tug-of-war between opposing parties who shared the same physical and occupational spaces. Sure, they worked together for the common agenda, but that was the end of their similarities. Everything else was disputable from pay to schedules and benefits to rights or privileges. They could agree on the common goal of getting the job done, but they could not agree on the methods, strategies, background arrangements or anything else that made it conducive for both parties to do their part and actually do the work.

This has been my primary focus for years---seeing to it that people understand each other's viewpoints. They begin to find common ground, compromise, and establish a working relationship. Both parties can become satisfied. Sometimes my work takes just a few hours. Sometimes, I deal with the back-and-forth disputing for months. Either way, I've never walked away from the table with a situation that has been closed as "unresolved". Why? Because I understand the fundaments of dispute resolution, negotiation and bringing disputants together. I have never forsaken those principles, regardless of the occupation, industry, or area in which I've worked.

I've seen tremendous success in executing the art of dispute resolution and negotiation. I've received plaques, accolades, and news clippings to prove it. However, I've learned that there's a bigger picture besides resolving conflicts for others. The bigger picture is that I must use my skill to teach people how to resolve conflicts for themselves.

One of the main miscommunication issues comes from the fact that we don't teach people how to resolve conflicts. In fact, we actually teach them how to create them. Society is very much the blame for many of the day-to-day disputes that arise between people. The subliminal messages we receive, the jealousy over materialistic things, the ability to avoid having meaningful conversations, the ability to spread misinformation at the speed of lightening without being held accountable for the fallacies, the ability to text what we feel and think instead of sitting down face-to-face to express ourselves-all of these things contribute to our inability to solve problems. Why? Because society has made it very easy and very acceptable to sweep things under the rug and avoid tough conversations.

Why Are We Arguing in the First Place?

When we begin to rationalize why disputes exist, we can learn that disputes don't exist due to differences in personality. They exist because of our behaviors. Our behaviors dictate our responses to the situations we find ourselves in. When we respond to a dispute with negative behaviors such as animosity, pigheadedness, anger or greed, these disputes become very difficult to solve.

Disputes start and also become harder to resolve because, in general, people bring a lot of emotional and mental baggage to the table. Although we'd like to think that we're arguing about one subject, the baggage we bring into these arguments fuels the fire for us to argue with such passion and indignant attitudes that sometimes we forget why we're arguing in the first place.

In my years of sitting at a table, in the middle of two opposing parties, I've realized that neither side chooses to acknowledge the other side's turmoil. No one knows what the other person or group of people are dealing with. There's no sense of compassion or understanding. Yes, it's a bit more difficult to do a professional setting. However, humanity trumps professional settings. Common respect trumps all disputes. There's an idiom that says, "in order to get respect you've have got to give respect". For this to be the case, we have to learn to tame the beast that dictates how much respect we give and receive and that ultimately determines how far a dispute will go---the ego.

While I am the professional neutral at one side of the table, willing to mediate/negotiate and use every tool in my professional arsenal to settle a dispute. Two very large egos are also at the table, unwilling to loosen their grips. Egos build tremendous momentum for disputes, allowing them to grow. It becomes more dangerous and impactful and goes without resolution for however long it takes. To make matters worse, sometimes the actual dispute can easily be resolved. The ego won't let it be over until someone feels as if they've won.

In addition to the unspoken or disregarded baggage, the ego creates this power struggle in a dispute. Oddly enough, during conflict, it's often not about who's right or who's wrong, because, generally speaking, people don't argue the facts. People argue and disagree because they feel that they should be dominating the rights on the subject. They want to control the yeses and no's or the "how much's" and "how often". They want to exude power. They want to have their way.

So, why are we arguing? Well, because we haven't yet learned how to understand our behavioral triggers. On any given day, we bring emotional baggage to the table to sit with us while we're disputing. And as icing on the cake, we invite our egos to the negotiation table to throw tantrums and impede our progress towards amicable resolutions. Thus, my job becomes tougher to do. And the people who are trying to prove their points and get their ways tighten their grips on their sides of the rope during tug-of-war.

"Sticks and Stones May Break My Bones, but Words Will Never Hurt Me" Is a Fallacy

As children, we're taught to diffuse situations where people say harsh words using the rhyme, "Sticks and stone my break my bones, but words will never hurt me". The idea of this rhyme is that words aren't as powerful as weapons, therefore no matter which kinds of words are hurled in your direction, they shouldn't cause you harm. This, readers, is a big fat lie. Not only is it a lie, but it's also detrimentally misleading. It teaches people to listen to or absorb words with negative connotations and intentions as long as you learn how to build yourself strong enough to deflect them. This is a serious instance of "psychological violence."

Psychological violence can be defined as anything that someone willingly does to another person to cause mental and emotional harm. During an intense dispute or negotiation, words are used very precisely, with every intention of conveying clear points of frustration, anger, disappointment and of course, power. People want their words to hurt. They want people on the opposing side to feel the sting of their non-negotiable points and their unwillingness to compromise, apologize or be the bigger person. In instances where you can't put your hands on another person to show the complexity of your bruised feelings and ego, you want your words to hurt.

Brazen words with brutal effects stem from poor communication skills. When it comes to disputes, stronger and more effective communication skills can help remedy a conflict. The problem is, however, that people don't trust the communication process. They don't trust that the intentional listening, the mindful speaking, the tone, tongue, and timeliness of word choices will make a positive impact on how they resolve their disputes. Yes, effective communication is the most logical approach to reducing conflict, negotiating, and ending disputes, but truth be told, it's not always the quickest or most widely acceptable approach.

Today's fast-paced technological world drastically impacts effective communication. Not only can we say brazen words at lightning speed, but we can also say these things without being face-to-face, talking on the phone, or even being in the same time zone. Technology is increasing the speed of our communication but decreasing the quality of our communication. And when the quality of the way we communicate is impacted, the chances for disputes and conflict surges. The words which we speak, do have the power to hurt people. And sometimes, that's exactly what they're meant to do.

So, Now What? How Can We Resolve Our Disputes and End Our Conflicts?

This book was meant to do two things: (1) point out the problems that exist in our communication within multiple areas of our lives and (2) show you how to resolve them---almost like a professional. Upon reading this book, you will learn that whether your conflict is in a business setting, educational, romantic, religious, cultural, or personal, there's a very sound, smart, and simple method to resolving it. You'll discover that this system uses four foundational points, three pivotal moments, and six steps in order to reach an amicable resolve. And though it sounds like a hefty and long process, all of these interconnected parts can take anywhere from two hours to six months to execute and see results. It all depends on how badly you would like to solve your problem.

As I've mentioned, I've been in this business a long time. However, I've also been married for a long time, a parent for a long time, and an employee for a long time. I've been exposed to my fair share of disputes and conflicts, some of which I care to forget and others that I believe made me a better communicator. Regardless, whether or not I made my point, "settled" the dispute or maintained the relationship, I certainly learned a lot about myself, the people I associated with, and how to move on with my life after conflict.

Before I can begin to tell you how to resolve your conflicts or become a better problem solver, you'll need to know a bit more about yourself. As you recall, behavior is a key player in how disputes and conflicts arise. When you have a better idea about (1) who you are, (2) what your triggers are and (3) how you respond to certain situations, then you'll be able to create a more effective strategy for participating in and ultimately resolving your problems.

NATURE OF CONFLICT

As children and adults, most of us learn how to be adversarial in dealing with others more than we learn how to resolve conflicts between people. In our past, we have learned how to fulfill many of our needs through controlling, and sometimes hurting others as opposed to accepting people through recognizing their feelings and sense of purpose. Moreover, we are often unable to really understand what another person communicates to us and find ourselves, instead, overwhelmed by the need to protect our self-image against what we think others might be saying or thinking about us.

CAUSES OF CONFLICT

- *Differences in values, philosophy, goals, or objectives*
- *Differences of opinion*
- *Differences in perception*
- *Role pressures*
- *Simple misunderstandings*
- *Poor communication*
- *Inaccurate or insufficient communication*
- *Limited resources*
- *Fights of power/turf/control*

METHODS OF RESOLVING DISPUTES

Mediation is a voluntary dispute settlement process. The parties involved in a dispute utilize a trained, neutral party to assist them in reconciling their differences and reaching an agreement. The mediator has no authority to impose a settlement.

Arbitration: a third party, or "arbitrator," makes a decision for all parties involved. The decision is binding on the involved parties.

This process can result from voluntary agreement to arbitrate or can be required under the terms of an agreement or state law.

Negotiation is a process allowing parties dealing with conflict to jointly take action towards mutually amicable resolution.

Factfinding in this process, a person of panel or persons, not involved in the dispute, complies and reports facts and differing perceptions of facts. This may include formal hearings, interviews, and/or research. A report may provide the framework for parties to use in negotiations and may also contain recommendations for settlement. As with mediation, fact finding leaves the decision-making power with the parties.

CONFLICT ANALYSIS OVERVIEW

Training sessions also provide participants with indispensable techniques necessary to perform CONFLICT ANALYSIS. Through education, negotiations, fact finding and arbitration, they have the tools required to utilize all areas of conflict resolution.

The major steps participants will learn in CONFLICT ANALYSIS are:

- *Determine the nature of the dispute.*
- *Identify who should and/or shouldn't be involved in the dispute.*
- *Identify the key decision maker and the roles others play in the dispute.*
- *Identify the points of agreement and disagreements.*
- *Identify the incentives to settle or the results of not settling the conflict.*
- *Identify the various approaches to resolving the conflict, including strategies and techniques.*
- *Consider parts of the dispute that the parties can and cannot resolve. Identify possible resources available to aid in the resolution of the conflict.*

Hez Brown & Associates, LLC
Conflict Resolution Training Center

CONFLICT RESOLUTION
WHAT IS IT AND WHY IS IT IMPORTANT?

Research shows over 85% of employees experience workplace conflict due to stress, workload, or personal clashes. As a result, companies lose approximately 2.8 hours each week resolving disputes, amounting to $359 billion in hours paid.

On the contrary, companies that utilize effective conflict resolution tactics and promote a healthy corporate culture reduce their turnover rate from 48.4% to 13.9%. Furthermore, 95% of people agree that conflict resolution is critical to promoting a happy and healthy culture and ensuring you act during disputes.

Conflict resulting involves managing and resolving conflicts between individuals, groups, and organizations to prevent disputes from escalating or spilling into violence. Conflict resolution entails various strategies, such as arbitration, negotiation, mediation, etc.

But using conflict resolution to solve disputes and build strong relationships can be tricky. Effective conflict resolution requires constant effort, from learning the right strategies to developing the necessary skills. Learn more about conflict resolution's definition, different types, benefits, and examples by reading on:

WHAT IS CONFLICT RESOLUTION?

Let's cover the **conflict resolution** definition before diving into its nitty-gritty:

Conflict is inevitable, aggravated by innumerable factors like stress, frustration, or even competitiveness. The disagreements might occur between employees, family members, volunteers, committee members, clients, or organizations.

Conflict resolution is an effective way for opposing parties to find a middle ground and identify a peaceful solution to their disputes. Resolving disputes and disagreements requires a complex skill set and an understanding of how to reconcile emotions.

Types of Conflict Resolution

Conflict resolution may vary depending on the unique situation and people involved. Let's discuss the three common types:

ASSERTIVENESS

In either care, assertiveness requires the following conflict-resolution skills:

- *Articulation*
- *Decisiveness*
- *Firmness*
- *Leadership*
- *Managing Emotions*
- *Negotiation*
- *Problem-Solving*
- *Socializing*
- *Stress Management*
- *Voicing Opinions*

EMPATHY

A third party might encourage empathy by asking the two people involved in a conflict to describe how the other might feel and think. Therefore, motivating them to assess the situation from the lens of the opposition party.

Empathy is also critical for the negotiator or mediator, who must understand each party's perspective. In this type of conflict resolution, the resolver must have the following skills:

- *Acquiring and Giving Feedback*
- *Compassion*
- *Identifying non-verbal cues*
- *Inclusion*
- *Interpersonal skills*
- *Managing Emotions*
- *Patience*
- *Personable*
- *Recognizing Differences*
- *Self-Control*
- *Self-Awareness*
- *Welcoming Opinions*

INTERVIEW AND ACTIVE LISTENING

Interviewing and active listening often involve a mediator or supervisor who asks questions and listens carefully to determine the nature of a conflict. After that, they might suggest helpful ways for the two people engaged in a dispute to solve and move past it.

Here are several conflict resolution skills necessary for this:

- *Attentiveness*
- *Conscientiousness*
- *Consideration*
- *Empathy*
- *Encouragement*
- *Listening*
- *Negotiation*
- *Presentation*
- *Relationship Building*
- *Sense of Humor*
- *Socializing*
- *Verbal and Non-Verbal Communication*

Why is Conflict Resolution Important?

Contrary to popular belief, ignoring a dispute will not make it go; instead, it might worsen, causing it to become highly destructive.

However, solving a conflict before is escalates can reap many benefits, including reducing stress, building deep relations, and help achieve common goals. Here we discuss the primary causes of disputes and the benefits of conflict resolution.

What Causes Conflicts

Here are the three common factors leading to conflicts among loved ones, employees, and organizations:

Misunderstandings

Misunderstandings are one of the most prevalent causes of conflict. It might arise from misinterpreting the following:

- _The nature and objective of a job_
- _The difference in values, beliefs or needs._
- _Expectations about how someone should do a task!_
- _Work conditions and wages_

Poor Communication

Effective communication relies on sending and receiving clear and complete messages. You can solve most relationship and organizational problems by focusing on the message's clarity. Both parties communicating are responsible for ensuring they consider these issues before sending a message.

Luckily, streamlining personal and workplace communication is not as challenging as it sounds. Here are several actionable tips:

- _Hold regular staff/management meetings to promote better communication and transparency._
- _Create a work-life balance to ensure you're giving time to your loved ones._
- _Give everyone tome to talk and voice their opinions._
- _Listen more than you talk._

Frustration And Stress

Feeling frustrated, stressed, or exhausted can increase your irritability, thus leading to increased conflicts. Therefore, you must recognize the signs of workplace or personal stress to prevent burnout.

Try to help people pinpoint the underlying cause of stress and take steps to combat these factors. Sometimes, stress and frustration might arise due to the following things:

- _Criticism and lack of management_

- *Continual Crises*
- *Dirty or untidy workspace*
- *Harassment*
- *Noise*
- *Overcrowding or lack of privacy and personal space*
- *Poor communication*
- *The tension between family members/staff members*

REASONS TO SOLVE CONFLICTS

Conflict resolution aims to help two people reach a satisfying, beneficial agreement. But there are several other reasons to resolve a workplace or personal dispute:

To learn more about those with different ideas, beliefs, and backgrounds: Resolving a conflict requires you to look at the argument from the other person's perspective.

To continue building a relationship with the opponent: If you find a peaceful solution with your opponent, you ensure that your relationships continue to grow and flourish.

To find peaceful solutions to challenging situations: Disputes that escalate require time, energy, motivation, and a good reputation. Negotiating and finding a solution can help protect these resources while make new allies!

BENEFITS OF CONFLICT RESOLUTION

Now, let's dive into the benefits of **conflict resolution:**

Build Strong Relationships

Personal and professional relationships can suffer due to unresolved arguments, leading to feelings of resentment or explosive behaviors.

Effective conflict resolution is the key to reducing discontent that could damage relationships and facilitates better collaboration.

Moreover, communication, emotional awareness, and empathy are crucial for conflict resolutions that encourage strong, long-lasting, and productive relationships between people.

Helps Achieve Goals

Resolving a conflict can help the people involved be more productive and work towards achieving common goals.

After a resolution, they can utilize conflict resolution skills, such as compromising, negotiating, and compassion, to increase efficiency.

Enhances Commitment

Conflict resolution teaches the people engaged in a dispute to tackle the problem as a team rather than each other. Therefore, it brings people together, enhances commitment, and helps mitigate feelings of defensiveness.

While conflicts can disrupt relationships, they also signify strong commitment and emotional attachment. By tapping into these feelings, each party can better understand the other one's goals, feelings, and thinking. As a result, conflict resolution can boost dedication and loyalty.

Promotes Active Listening

Active listening is a critical skill, regardless of your profession. In conflict resolution, no strategy will work if you don't actively listen to what the other person is saying.

Therefore, to listen actively, you must put your assumptions aside, keep an open mind, ask questions, and respond to people using their words. Disagreements often escalate because people don't pay attention and wait for their turn to speak.

However, by promoting active listening, conflict resolution can reduce future disputes.

What are the FIVE Best Conflict Resolution Strategies?

Conflict resolution is reaching an agreement for a dispute that satisfies everyone involved. When addressing a conflict, there are various strategies you can follow.

Here we'll discuss the five conflict resolution strategies that ensure a positive outcome from disputes:

COGNITIVE ERRORS TO CONSIDER

Successful conflict resolutions involve being self-aware and recognizing mistakes while resolving conflicts. Having this knowledge and correcting them can significantly improve the conflict resolution process.

So, before we discuss the different conflict resolution strategies, let's dig deeper into the common mistakes people take:

PSYCHOANALYZING

Often, we believe that we know what the other person is thinking and feeling based on our interpretations of their actions. The worst part? The assumptions are always negative.

As a result, psychoanalyzing and mind-reading the opposition party can ruin your relationship and create hostility. Instead, try asking about their feelings.

OVERCONFIDENCE

Overconfidence is another common mistake people make when arguing or disputing a matter. While this element only leads to embarrassment in personal disagreement, it can be detrimental to legal issues.

Furthermore, overconfidence can prevent you from understanding the other person's perspective, thus preventing you and the opposition from reaching a solution.

OVER GENERALIZING

Sometimes, when a situation doesn't match our values or expectations, we blow it out of proportion by over-generalizing.

Instead of starting sentences with, "You always" or "You never," take a step back and identify whether what you believe is accurate. Furthermore, bringing up past conflicts to stir up negativity is counterproductive. It will only worsen the situation and prevent you from finding common ground.

SELF-SERVING FAIRNESS INTERPRETATIONS

"Self-serving fairness interpretations" involve one or more people deciding what is "fair" from a biased perspective. Unfortunately, this can lead to further misunderstandings and ruin relationships.

Therefore, conflict resolution requires you to discuss the dispute from a neutral stance.

FORGETTING TO LISTEN

Some people make faces, roll their eyes, interrupt, and decide what to say next instead of actively listening to the other person. Unless you make an effort to understand your opposition party, you won't reach a satisfying and beneficial solution.

Therefore, listening to the other person with an open mind is essential.

MAKING CHARACTER ATTACKS

Lastly, making character attacks is a common and destructive cognitive error that disrupts conflict resolution flow.

When one of more people resort to inflicting emotional damage, it creates a hostile discussion environment and negative perceptions. Therefore, respecting the other person is critical, as avoiding making low blows.

Top Five Conflict Resolution Strategies

There are five common strategies to resolve conflicts you can try in the workplace or at home:

1. **NEGOTIATION**

   Negotiating can be tricky, but it's vital to solving a conflict. Negotiating a situation requires you to put your differences aside and work together to reach a peaceful conclusion. It can also encourage you to build relationships because it shows that you're willing to put your ideals aside to find a satisfying solution.

   Furthermore, successfully negotiating a situation can help improve efficiency, commitment, and dedication.

2. **MEDIATION**

   Having a mediator is one of the most common yet effective ways of solving workplace and personal conflicts. This strategy includes a neutral third party who can help both parties empathize with each other while voicing their opinions.

   Involving a mediator can offer you unbiased opinions on the situation, thus helping you provide answers based on facts, not personal feelings. Ultimately, it enables you to find a beneficial solution.

3. **COMPROMISING**

   Compromising or reconciling seeks a mutual agreement to solve a personal or workplace dispute. In this case, both parties willingly forfeit several conditions to reach a solution.

   Compromising is an effective way of resolving conflicts before they escalate and become destructive. Furthermore, it can be temporary solution until the parties implement a permanent one.

4. AVOIDING

As the name suggests, avoiding involves ignoring the conflict to avoid engaging in it. Moreover, avoiding allows them to forget that a problem exists.

In most cases, avoiding it is not a viable option. But sometimes, when there is no clear solution, or both parties need time before the confrontation, avoiding can improve communication.

5. LITIGATION

In severe conflicts, litigation might be the best solution. In this strategy, both parties will go before a judge or jury.

Next, the judge will listen to their argument, weigh the evidence, and then make a fair and unbiased decision. The judge/jury might be anyone who is not directly involved in the conflict.

SIX CONFLICT RESOLUTION SKILLS

You'll need to develop complex skills to manage and mitigate conflicts successfully. Below are six skills that are crucial for resolving disputes:

1. Problem-Solving

Problem-solving in terms of conflict resolution involves the pursuit of alternative solutions that satisfy the needs and goals of both parties.

It starts with prioritizing the conflict instead of trying to be "right."

2. Emotional Intelligence

Emotional intelligence is the capacity to sense and understand the emotions of others as well as your own. It is crucial for conflict management since it stops things from getting worse. Communicating with your opponent without provoking them will be simpler if you can accurately read their feelings.

Everyone concerned may think sensibly and creatively about a solution when the parties acknowledge the disagreement's perplexity, rage, and irritation.

3. Collaboration

It's crucial to work together, find a middle ground, and compromise in a dispute because both parties think they're in the right. Collaboration ensures that all sides are heard, ensuring that the solution does not favor one party over another. Working together will also probably result in a quicker resolution. Collaboration involves putting aside your ego and working together to solve the current problem.

4. Positivity

An excellent strategy to keep the dialogue going in a conflict situation is to use positive conflict management techniques. Conflicts are full of barriers; if you want to settle, you must be eager to overcome them. By approaching the issue with a positive outlook, you might put other participants at rest who might be apprehensive about the interaction.

5. Remaining Calm

Our natural reaction during a disagreement is occasionally to give in to strong feelings like wrath and irritation, but this rarely leads to a compromise. Maintaining composure when resolving a problem is crucial because your tone of voice can significantly impact a dialogue. Even though it could be challenging, maintaining composure is essential to avoid escalating the conflict.

6. Not Playing the Blame Game

Placing blame on one another during a dispute is the last thing you want to do. Pointing fingers will only serve to aggravate the conflict and make things worse. Instead, provide a secure environment that avoids blaming any one individual.

Additionally, you should avoid taking the initiative because doing so could make it more challenging to discover a solution. Instead, everyone should have a fair opportunity to speak without silencing the other. Giving everyone a chance to express their emotions and ideas is essential.

Step-by-Step Guide to Resolve Conflict

To negotiate a conflict's resolution successfully, follow these steps:

Understanding The Conflict

Conflict can occur for a variety of causes. To win the argument, you must understand your opponent's interests and your own. Here are some inquiries you should make of yourself to describe the disagreement.

- *What do I find interesting?*
- *In this conflict, what matters to me most?*
- *What am I seeking?*
- *What am I lacking?*
- *What worries, hopes or fears do I have?*

Communicating With the Opposition

You can start talking to your opposition directly now that you've considered your interests and those of the other side. Here are some pointers for having productive conversations:

- *You value others' opinions because they are the cause of your disagreements. You must consider whether or not anything is significant to them. Of course, recognizing does not imply consent.*

- *Let everyone participate. A resolution will matter to all who take part. People look for a fair compromise.*

- *Express your intense feelings. Allow the opposing side to vent.*

- *However, avoid responding to emotional outbursts! Instead of shouting back, try saying sorry. There is no harm in apologizing, and it is frequently a successful strategy.*

- *Be firm but adaptable. Instead of discussing your position, talk about your interests.*

- *Avoid making snap decisions. Continue to seek out information and ask questions.*

- *Find a method to make their choice simple. Instead of calling it a method to "save face," try to find a way for them to accept your perspective without coming across as weak in negotiations, egos matter.*

BRAINSTORMING AND SELECTING RESOLUTIONS

You can begin formulating solutions now that you know the goals shared by the two parties and ways to interact with them more effectively. Search for similar interests among the claims you have mentioned for yourself and your opponents. Both sides frequently have many same interests. For instance, both parties may value stability and public respect.

Before a brainstorming session, think seriously about how you'll organize the gathering. For the meeting, create a clear purpose statement. Try to select a small group of no more than 5-8 people. Hold the meeting somewhere other than your specific location. Make sure the environment is relaxing and encouraging to feel safe. Find a neutral facilitator who can organize the meeting without expressing personal opinions regarding the disagreement.

EXPLORING ALTERNATIVES

Even with your best efforts and sincere intentions, there may be instances when you cannot resolve your issue. You should consider this possibility before launching into discussions. When will you decide to end negotiations? What other options do you have if you and your opponent cannot come to terms?

Early in the negotiation process, it's crucial to devise settlement choices; you should always keep your best option in the back of your mind. Compare your potential agreements with your opponent to this "best" option. You cannot negotiate if you don't know the alternative!

Start with brainstorming to come up with an alternative solution. After that, weigh the advantages and disadvantages of each option. Consider realistic and valuable alternatives. Consider how you may improve it as well.

THE BOTTOM LINE

There's no need to associate conflict with a frightening eight-letter word. We can improve our relationships and communicate our expectations regarding others' expectations by resolving disputes. You can choose when to avoid conflict and when to address it by comprehending the five conflict resolution techniques and putting those techniques into practice. It will improve your interactions with your coworkers and clients.

CHANGING NEGATIVE THINKING PATTERNS ABOUT CONFLICT

1. Change Adversity to Opportunity

2. Change Negative Belief to Positive Alternative

3. Change Reactive to Proactive

4. Change Awfulizing to Areas of Mutual Agreement

5. Change Procrastination to First Action Step

QUESTIONS TO ASK IN DIFFICULT SITUATIONS

1. What evidence do I have for my belief?

2. Are there alternative ways of looking at the adversity?

3. What are the implications of my belief?

4. What is the usefulness of my belief?

ONCE BOTH PARTIES AGREE TO RESOLVE THE CONFLICT

1. Listen carefully.

2. Define the apparent problems from two perspectives.

3. Invite joint problem-solving.

4. Design a specific problem-solving process which both parties agree on.

5. Restate the problem from the other party's point of view.

6. Brainstorm action alternatives.

7. Take action.

8. Develop system to monitor action taken, evaluate success and meet periodically to discuss other potential solutions to manage future conflicts more proactively.

Rules For Interactions

1. RESPECT EVERYONE DEEPLY.

2. IF YOU INTERACT WITH SOMEONE WHO YOU DO NOT THINK IS DESERVING OF DEEP RESPECT, REFER TO RULE NUMBER 1.

A QUICK REVIEW OF
CONFLICT MANAGEMENT

- Acknowledge that it is OK to disagree.

- Acknowledge the emotional issues.

- Listen actively.

- Identify areas of agreement

- Clarify the difference of opinion – rely on facts.

- Discuss the value of different viewpoints.

- Understand the difference and reason for them.

- Put yourself in the other person's position.'

- Be open minded.

- Use problem solving.

- Generate many potential solutions.

- Try to extract the best attributes of each conflicting idea.

- Keep the conflict focused on opinions and facts, not people.

Conflict Resolution in Classrooms
Could Curb Violence

The United States of America is the most advanced and powerful nation in the world when it comes to military preparedness, advanced technology, economics, and standard of living. With a few exceptions, we are holding our own and can compete globally in every area.

One area where we fall far short and lack any strategic plans for improvement is in our response to physical and psychological violence. We are fundamentally unable to grasp the essence and root causes of violence, and this prohibits us from seeking the appropriate solutions when dealing with violence and race relations.

Physical violence such as assault, rape, or murder is an extreme form of aggression. It's behavior in which physical force is exerted for the purpose of causing damage or injury. Psychological violence is anything that an individual or group does to knowingly harm others, be it verbally, mentally, morally, racially, criminally, sexually, or emotionally. Psychological violence is by and large rendered with the tongue; timing and tone can be as devastating as physical violence. The physically strongest person can be adversely injured by words.

In fact, gun violence is one of the deadliest components of violence. Approximately ninety individuals are gunned down through gun violence daily. Meanwhile, segregation and discrimination are rampant and appear to be acceptable as a way of life. We have the haves against the have-nots, whites against blacks, blacks against whites, rich against poor, males against females, religion against religion, young against old. All these conflicts are a form of violence.

Obviously, there is a reason for our failure in these areas. In my opinion, the basic reason for our failures and our reluctance to address these complex issues is, simply put, economics. Addressing this phenomenon is going to cost money, and most institutions are unwilling to make the investments.

In fact, our country is home to some of the most prestigious colleges and universities, each doing an excellent job preparing students for the world of work. However, we fail miserably when it comes to teaching our children how to manage conflict and deal with diversity. We fail to formally teach our children and advanced students how to manage and solve problems beyond the academic ones they encounter in the classroom. Managing conflict is a skill that can be taught to children and adults. Learning to solve conflict is like learning to swim or ride a bicycle. Once learned, you never forget it. Just think: children are not born violent. Violence is a learned behavior, and children by and large become a product of their environment. Children are not born hating others who don't look, or worship like them. This hatred is taught to them as they grow up and is passed along from generation to generation – similar to a rite of passage – by their elders for no rational reason other than meanness.

This behavior has now spilled over into all segments of our society, even politics, where it is now fashionable to stereotype individuals because of their religion, race, sex, sexual orientation, or nation's origin. This happens without any consequences, compassion, or feeling for those adversely affected by it.

In my opinion, one of the methods available to address the problem is within our reach. I believe that learning the humanistic approach to problem-solving at an early age is essential to our society's success and will ultimately save lives and money. Many of those who are incarcerated possibly could have avoided going to prison had they been taught some basic skills in resolving conflict. These skills could have been taught in our schools since most children are not taught problem-solving skills at home. Managing conflict and diversity should be a mandatory part of the school curriculum because it will better prepare our children for the real world. Children need to be taught the importance of self-examination, forgiveness, apology, compassion, and developing good listening skills in order to become a holistic person.

Because of the size of the problem and the limitation on teachers and administrators in terms of discipline, there has to be a different approach. I believe that in order to address this critical problem, every school district should implement a mandatory conflict-resolution training program for grades K-12. I recognize that there are costs involved. I also realize this recommendation is not the ultimate panacea. However, if implemented in our schools, a conflict-resolution training program would pay tremendous dividends, ultimately saving lives and money and, in some instances, preventing incarceration.

Bullying and Gang and Gun Violence
"So What?"

I decided to offer a few solutions and recommendations on how to address this global issue. It has a devastating impact on our schools and communities on a daily basis. I was further motivated to write this book after reading the local newspapers and watching the local television report the news regarding gun violence, gangs, and bullying. In fact, there is hardly a single day that passes in which we do not hear of young children and adults being killed or wounded by gunfire. Just this past week, it was reported that a four-year-old child was attending service and was hit by a stray bullet. It is time for us as a community to start to take some action in assisting in eradicating the problem. If not now, when? If not us, who?

Somehow, these advances seem to escape the various communities, especially in our schools and minority communities. Violence, bullying, and conflict seem to be a way of life in our schools. Our children seem to lack the social skills needed to handle and manage these issues. Let's take a look at bullying, for example—a pervasive issue in our schools. Recent statistics around bullying are frightening:

- 8% of students miss one day of school per month.
- 43% fear harassment in school bathrooms.
- 80% of the time, arguments with a bully result in physical altercations.
- 30% of students heard another student threaten to kill someone.
- 20% of students know of other students who bring guns to school.
- Every seven minutes, a child is bullied, increasing violence on school grounds.

- Each month, 282,000 students are physically attacked in schools.
- Most of the violence actually occurs on school ground.

Analyzing this data produces frightening revelations. Our children are losing the battle. They are on the front line of the American social conflict.

I believe that by teaching young people the values associated with managing conflict, we address other issues that may be lacking. We should teach children the values of compassion, forgiveness, and the humility associated with the art of apologizing for behavior that negatively affects others.

Most of us send our child (or minors that we care for) to school. We help them with their homework, attend the parent-teacher conferences, go to their ceremonies, and do all the things we're supposed to do when it comes to preparing them to become great students. As parents or guardians, we understand the importance of education. We try to shape their minds and motivate them to understand the importance of their education as well.

There's nothing wrong with being the parent that sends their child to school to learn and become the best thinker that they can become. However, school is not just a place of learning and churning out assignments. School is also a place for social engagement and developing relationship-building skills. It's one of the places where a child's character begins to form and where they experience the most social pressure and mental development. School is beyond the books and the projects. School is where your child learns how to deal with a variety of people of different ages, backgrounds, and personality types who live in their community.

Our children are interacting with adults and their peers for at least seven hours a day, five days a week. You would think we'd pay extra attention to the quality of those encounters and teach them how to deal with conflict. However, this is not the case. Most children don't learn how to deal with conflict until they are facing it or after it's already happened. So, while they're at school learning reading, writing, and arithmetic, they're also probably encountering conflict. This would be in the form of bullying, losing friends, not fitting in, or not properly respecting their authoritative figures. Yet if they come home with good grades and merit awards, as parents or guardians, we may not notice the problem until it's too late.

It would be nice to think that childhood conflict doesn't appear in school-aged children until secondary school or later. However, this is a fallacy. From the moment we drop our children off at school for the very first time, we are placing them in situations where they will not only face academic challenges, but they'll also face social challenges. While some challenges may be greater than others and not all challenges will warrant extreme disciplinary action, the fact is, these challenges may turn into conflicts. And our children rarely know how to deal with those conflicts.

To take it a step further, early on in life, children learn the chant "Sticks and stones may break my bones, but words will never hurt me." This couldn't be farther from the truth. This chant has good intentions, but honestly, it doesn't actually speak to or even remotely resolve the hurt feelings, anger, and frustration that our children feel when their peers taunt them with maleficent words. In fact, hurtful speech is one of the biggest acts of psychological violence that our children endure during their early childhood education. The amount of teasing and taunting that goes on during a school day is more than enough for their fragile minds and emotions to deal with. Yet we don't actually teach them how to deal with these threats to their social development and personal happiness. Instead, most of us resort to the same old chant of "Sticks and stones may break my bones, but words will never hurt me."

We should be teaching them that words do hurt sometimes. While we can't let these words stop us from pursuing greater things, we do need to learn how to deal with hateful or emotionally draining speech. Furthermore, we need to teach them how to deal with the social, emotional, and physical conflicts that could arise from this type of speech. Teaching children to ignore the words only suppresses the need to respond. It doesn't help them identify, reply, and remedy the situation in a mature and amicable manner. And although you may be thinking "My five-year-old son/daughter wouldn't understand what that process means!" The truth is, they probably would.

We don't give our children enough credit for their ability to receive high-level information and process it according to their own maturity levels. Also, we don't take enough time to give them the information, even if it takes multiple attempts for them to understand it. They need help to process information according to their own maturity levels. So, what tends to happen is, we delay conversations, education, and training about conflict and dispute resolution. Unfortunately, we end up sitting in the principal's office, or worse, the police station, questioning how things got so bad and what could've been done to prevent this.

At the onset of their educational journeys, we should be teaching our children how to deal with people who think, behave, or speak indifferently toward them. We shouldn't be telling them to ignore it or get over it. Instead, we should be honest about how it makes them feel and how they should approach and respond to it. And yes, this can be taught to a child in preschool. In fact, have you ever observed young children (between the ages of three and five years old) engage with their peers? It can be one of the most joyful yet complex observances. The range in their emotions and interactions will show you that young children definitely need to learn how to resolve their own conflicts—especially before overprotective parents get involved. From snatching toys and not sharing to taunting, throwing tantrums, and being defiant, these traits are a part of self-expression and social development. Yet they're also an indicator that there's a conflict that the child hasn't been taught to handle.

Our children are automatically subjected to dealing with people and learning how to manage their relationships, yet they aren't taught what to do when a conflict occurs. We teach them how to play physically defend themselves at a young age (even going as far as showing them the proper way to hold their fists and land a punch). However, we don't do the prerequisite work of teaching them how to resolve their problems before they turn into physical altercations. To make matters worse, we'll defend our children in the principal's office or anywhere else then they've responded in a physical altercation, with statements such as "The other kid started it!" or "He/she was defending themselves during the attack!" However, how often do we hold ourselves accountable, or parents or guardians, and admit that had we taught them to resolve conflicts with maturity and level-headedness, perhaps none of this would've happened in the first place?

Think of it, fifteen minutes of "what to do to handle conflicts" dialogue and training results in seventy-five minutes of training per week. This adds up to about five hours of training per month and forty hours of training within a school year. It doesn't take away from the rest of their critical learning needs, but it can reduce the amount of time that teachers, administrators, and parents can spend with dealing with the grievances of a child who has been engaged in a conflict. It can reduce the amount of time teachers spend on breaking up fights and arguments. It can reduce the overhead expenses for security measures such as surveillance cameras, metal detectors, and security guards in the school. Fifteen minutes of conflict resolution education can prevent the physical, emotional, and social damages. This is usually caused by children not knowing how to deal with their conflicts because they haven't been taught.

In addition, those same fifteen minutes can be used at home. As parents, we can have conversations about how to respond to negative speech and actions—far beyond ignoring it or throwing up their fists. The unique thing about teaching our children about conflict resolution at home is that we can show our children, through their own behaviors and dialogue, what they should and should not be doing. The next time there's a sibling brawl, instead of taking sides, yelling, breaking up the fight, or punishing your children, ask them what happened and how they could've handled it differently. Walk them through the mediation process by establishing neutral ground (the kitchen table or your family room is a great place for this). Ask them to individually address their grievances, giving them both ample time to speak their minds and state the problem; but don't allow them to talk across the table or engage in a verb al brawl. Then ask them to explain how it made them feel or why they responded the way that they did. Ask them about what would make things better between them and how to execute those details. Finally, ask them to agree to the resolution or propose a different one. Once they agree on the resolution, not only has the problem been dealt with future conflicts using tried-and-true conflict resolutions approaches.

It's time to introduce conflict resolution into our children's regular education—in school and at home. We're living in an age where information spreads so quickly and our children are constantly stimulated and triggered by the programming from their electronic devices, entertainment, and peer pressure. Without proper conflict resolution training, especially within our children's regular learning routines, we're not preparing our children to be mature, responsible, well-meaning, and respectable children and then adults. We can no longer afford to tell them that words won't hurt them or to put up their fists, because words are increasingly becoming more hateful and traveling faster and farther with things like social media and text messages. And fists are the last things that kids are thinking about in a physical altercation—now they respond with weapons. A simple and intentional conversation and training on identifying, preventing, and ultimately resolving conflict resolution not only makes our children well-equipped people, but it could also help save their lives.

Another tool that should be used to reduce conflict in the schools, home and communities is peer mediation.

What is Peer Meditation?

Peer mediation is a process where trained students act as neutral mediators. These students work with their peers to uncover the root causes of their disputes and decide on fairways of resolving conflict. The process is great because it's a form or restorative discipline and helps students build their empathy while they also fine tune their problem-solving skills.

You have heard the phrase "judged by a jury of your peers", plenty of times in your life. It's a fundamental part of our judicial system: Our judgement will be handed down by people just like us. However, for many students, that same system doesn't apply. Students often get "judged" and "sentenced" by people much older than them. Mediation seeks to change that. Learning new skills every day. Just like you get into fights, scuffles or conflict with your co-worker, friends and family, students do too. Also, just like you, your students are perfectly capable of coming up with their own form of resolutions that aren't punishment-based.

Introduction to Peer Mediation

In peer mediation, a trained youth acts as neutral mediator helping parties in conflict to understand the root causes of their dispute and to ultimately agree on a plan for resolving the conflict. Each individual mediation consists of six distinct stages:

1. Agree to Mediate

2. Storytelling and Gathering Points of View

3. Focus on Interests and Needs

4. Create Win-Win Solutions

5. Evaluate Options

6. Create an Agreement

The introduction of peer mediation programs in schools and community-serving organizations is based on a model of education that empowers individuals to prevent, resolve, and transform violent and nonviolent conflict by developing the values, attitudes, skills, and knowledge to envision alternative options for action towards building peace.

Benefits of Peer Mediation

Evidence shows that peer mediation fosters self-regulation, self-esteem, and self-discipline in youth (Johnson & Johnson 1997; Turnuklu et al., 2010). Another positive outcome of peer mediation training is the ability of trained youth to transfer mediation skills to a variety of settings including family and neighborhood conflicts, helping youth to become better problem-solvers and more responsible citizens (Johnson & Johnson 1996b; Turnuklu, et al., 2010). Research supports the finding that a sense of belonging is a very important factor in preventing violence in schools. Suspension or expulsion can push students further away from their learning communities whereas a school peer mediation program promotes critical thinking and builds decision-making skills, develops healthy standards of relationship within the school community and support student self-determination.

Conflicts of different intensity levels are an everyday occurrence between people everywhere. When parties to a conflict do not know how to communicate openly and honestly, the conflict tends to escalate and grow. Peer mediation programs provide youth and adults with the tools and skills to resolve conflicts nonviolently.

PEER Mediation and the Youth Leadership for Peace Project

IREX and partner organization Foundation for Tolerance International (FTI) created the Conflict Prevention and Peer Mediation Toolkit to support the creation of peer mediation programs at schools in Kyrgyzstan as part of the Youth Leadership for Peace Project funded by the United States Institute of Peace (USIP). After receiving training on conflict prevention, peer mediation, and use of the Toolkit, teachers, and youth from the Batken and Chui regions of Kyrgyzstan initiated peer mediation programs at 16 schools. From January – June 2013, peer mediator held more than 60 mediations, with 90% of mediations resulting in a signed mediation agreement.

Guide to Using the Toolkit:

In this Toolkit, you will find the training notes, handouts, sample agendas, and resource templates needed to initiate a peer mediation program for youth.

INTENDED AUDIENCE:

The resources in this Toolkit were initially developed for use by teachers and youth in Kyrgyzstan and are designed for an audience for youth ages 13-18. Activities can be adapted for a younger or older audience.

GETTING STARTED:

Beginning a peer mediation program in a school or community-serving organization requires the commitment of a core group of youth and adults who are motivated to learn peer mediation methodology and to serve as neutral and confidential mediators.

A peer mediation program will be most successful when anchored by.

1. active involvement of youth participants in the planning and implementation of the program,

2. a supportive adult or group of adults that is motivated to manage the program together with youth leaders, and

3. a supportive organization, such as a school or community youth center, to provide a physical space for mediations and encourage students or youth center patrons to use the mediation service.

PREPARATION NOTES FOR TRAINERS:

Before carrying out any of the trainings in this Toolkit, trainers are encouraged to design a training plan for preparing new mediators. Two sample training plans are included here. Prior to each training course, trainers should prepare the necessary supplies and handouts according to the training notes and consider how each training can be best adapted to meet the needs of the training participants. Because discussion of conflict can elicit strong emotions, trainers should be prepared to provide emotional support to participants and to direct participants to school and community resources for additional psychological support.

Sample Fourteen Week Training Plan

Depending on how many hours per week are available for training, you may decide to implement your peer mediation training program over an extended period of weekly meeting or an intensive multi-day training.

The following is a suggested plan for splitting up the training sessions in this Toolkit over a period of fourteen weeks.

Week One: What is Conflict?
Conflict is..

Dimensions of Conflict

Peace is…

Week Two:
Responses to Conflict

How I Respond to Conflict

Week Three:
Basic Needs

How I Meet My Basic Needs

Week Four:
Resources – Enough is Not Enough

Different Values

Conflict Outcomes

Week Five:
What is Mediation?

Stages of Mediation

A Successful Peer-Mediation

A Peer-Mediator is..

To be a Peer-Mediator is to be a Leader.

Week Six:
Agree to mediate.

Sample Script of Mediation Opening

Week Seven:

Communication

Active Listening

Summarizing

Week Eight:
"I" Messages

Communication Inhibitors

Clarifying Statements and Questions

Week Nine:
Restating and Repeating in Your Words What You Heard

Skills for Effective Communication

Week Ten:
Storytelling and Gathering Difference Points of View Perspectives

Week Eleven:
Dealing with Emotions

Feelings Inventory

Getting Your Buttons Pushed During Mediation

Week Twelve:
Positions/Interests/Needs

Focus on Interests and Needs

Week Thirteen:
Brainstorming and Evaluating Options

Create Win-Win Solutions

Week Fourteen:
What is Fair?

Create an Agreement

Putting It All Together

Sample Intensive Training Plan

Another option is to concentrate much of the mediation training on a two- or three-day intensive seminar, and to continue meeting weekly to cover the rest of the material. The following is a sample training agenda for a three-day peer mediation training seminar.

Day One – Sources of Conflict

TIME	Session Name	Activity Description
8:00 – 9:00	Getting to Know Each Other	-Icebreakers - Participants' expectations - Orientation - Agreeing on Rules
9:00 – 10:30	What is Conflict?	- Conflict Is… - Dimensions of Conflict
BREAK		
11:00 – 12:00	Active Listening	- Active listening (Summarizing, Asking Clarifying Questions)
12:00 – 1:00	Dealing with Emotions	
LUNCH		
1:30 – 2:30	First Stage of Mediation – Opening	- What is Mediation? - Stages of Mediation - Agree to Meditate
2:30 – 3:00	Closing Activity	Summary + Closing Game

Day Two – The Mediation Process

TIME	Session Name	Activity Description
8:00 – 8:45	Icebreaker Review of First Day	
8:45 – 9:45	Second Stage of Mediation – Storytelling	- Storytelling and Gathering Perspectives

	BREAK	
10:00 – 12:30	Third Stage of Mediation – Positions, Interests and Needs	- Basic Needs - How I Meet My Basic Needs - Resources – Enough is Not Enough - Different Values - Positions/Interests/Needs
	LUNCH	
1:30 – 2:30	First Stage of Mediation – Opening	- What is Mediation? - Stages of Mediation - Agree to Meditate
2:30 – 3:00	Closing Activity	Summary + Closing Game

Day Three – Practice

TIME	**Session Name**	**Activity Description**
8:00 – 8:45	Icebreaker Review of First & Second Days	
8:45 – 9:45	Fifth Stage of Mediation – Evaluate Options	- Brainstorming and Evaluating Options
	BREAK	
10:00 – 11:00	Sixth Stage of Mediation – Positions, Interests and Needs	- What is Fair? - Create an Agreement
11:00 – 1:00	Role Play Full Mediation	
	LUNCH	
1:30 – 2:30	Review	
2:30 – 3:00	Closing Activity	

INTRODUCTION TO THE MEDIATION PROCESS

Purpose:

- To introduce the six stages of mediation.
- To become familiar with the flow of the mediation process.

Length: 30 minutes

Number of Participants:

Materials: Flipchart, The Stages of Peer Mediation Handout

Procedure:

1. Explain that now that we have gotten a better understanding of both conflict and peace, we are going to learn the actual process of mediation as a tool for resolving conflicts.

2. Explain that there are six stages in the mediation process we will be learning, and we will be learning them step-by-step.

3. Have seven sheets of flipchart paper taped to the wall. The first sheet should have the title "Six Stages of Mediation" and the six steps listed below:

    1. Agree to Mediate
    2. Storytelling and Gathering Points of View
    3. Focus on Interests and Needs
    4. Create Win-Win Solutions
    5. Evaluate Options
    6. Create an Agreement

4. On the next flipchart sheet, write the name of the first step of mediation: **1. Agree to Mediate.**

   Ask the participants what they think happens during this stage of the mediation. Write down the responses. Make sure to elicit the following:

   - Sets the stage for mediation and establishes trust.

   - Introductions (all participants in the mediation introduce themselves).

   - Sets the ground-rules for the mediation.

   - Provides the participants with the logistics of the mediation (length, how it works).

5. On the next sheet, write the name of the second stage of mediation: **2. Storytelling and Gathering Points of View.** Repeat the process of asking the participants what they think happens during this stage and writing down their answers. Make sure to elicit the following:

   - Each participant has the opportunity to tell his or her side of the conflict.

   - The mediators use their active listening skills (empathizing, asking questions, summarizing, etc.)

6. Continue to the next sheet – **3. Focus on Interests and Needs.** Same process, make sure to elicit the following:

   - The stage allows the mediator to uncover the interests and needs that lie beneath the stated positions.

   Place this sheet very close to the Storytelling sheet and draw a curved arrow on the Storytelling sheet and the other half on the Focus on Interests and Needs sheet to indicate that these stages are less linear and often merge and go back and forth.

   Point out that these two stages are usually the heart of the mediation process and often require patience and skill.

7. Move on to the next stage: **4. Create Win-Win Solutions.** Ask the participants to recall the different kinds of outcomes that are possible in conflict situations (Lose-Lose, Win-Lose, Win-Win), the ultimate goal of mediation is to help the parties reach a win-win solution, so that both of their needs are met. Make sure to elicit:

   - Parties will brainstorm possible solutions for the conflict, with the help of mediators.

   - This stage is about creative problem-solving.

8. Move on to the next stage: **5. Evaluate Options.** Once the parties have brainstormed possible solutions, make sure to elicit:

   - Mediators help participants to evaluate the different options.

   Point out that this stage is more practical and pragmatic, but it also represents a turning point in the conflict; the parties are no longer working against each other but are instead working together to resolve the conflict.

9. Finally, the last stage is 6. Reaching an Agreement. Ask the participants what an agreement is, what types there are (verbal, written) and what one would normally find in an agreement. Elicit the following:

   - The names of the participants (who)

   - What they agree to do or not do (what)

   - The timeline (when)

   - The place (where)

   Specific details about the implementation of the agreement (how).

Ask the participants what role the mediator should play during this stage and point out that as the problem belongs to the participants, the agreement must come from them and belong to them as well. The agreement is a combination of ideas that were raised during the previous two stages and ultimately must be something that both sides can and do agree to. As mediators, our role is to make sure that the agreement is specific and that both sides feel that it is fair.

10. Summarize by repeating the stages and reminding the participants that we will be learning more about each stage in depth.

A Successful Peer-Mediation

✓ Is friendly.
✓ Wants to help others and cares about others resolving their conflicts.
✓ Show no prejudice.
✓ Is impartial and does not take side in the conflict.
✓ Is a good listener.
✓ Takes in all facts.
✓ Shows empathy.
✓ Knows when to be a leader.
✓ Helps each party to see the other's perspective.

A Peer-Mediator...

IS	IS NOT
A good listener	1. A disciplinarian
2. A team player	2. A boss
3. A fair person	3. A judge
4. A helper	4. An advice giver
5. Dependable	5. A gossip
6. Trustworthy	6. Dishonest
7. Compassionate	7. A therapist

To Be a Peer-Mediator is to be a Leader

Purpose:

- To better understand the characteristics of a leader and to get a picture of the qualities that make up respected leaders.

- To put peer-mediation in a leadership context so that the participants begin to see themselves as leaders in their school/communities.

Length: 30 – 45 minutes

Number of Participants: 4 or more

Materials: flipchart, markers

Procedure:

1. Ask the participants "If you could sit down for a cup of coffee with any leader from any period in history, man, or woman, real or fictional, political, cultural, social, personal, spiritual, etc., who would it be, and why?

2. As the participants go around the circle, each one to try and elaborate on it is exactly that makes the person they chose a leader: What qualities do/did they possess? What behavior do/did they exhibit? Were they chosen, or did they become leaders because of certain circumstances? As they answer, write down the key words and phrases that you hear on the flipchart/whiteboard.

3. Further questions for discussion:
   - What kinds of leaders are there? What types of leadership styles? (Formal – autocratic/authoritarian, democratic/participatory, inherited; non-Formal – teachers, artists, managers, parents, etc.)

- What is the difference between positive leadership and negative leadership? Is there such a thing? How can we know if someone is a positive or a negative leader?

- Are leaders born or molded? Can the traits that we identified be learned and acquired, or does one have to be born with them? Can we all be leaders?

- How do you see yourselves as leaders? How can peer-mediators be meaningful leaders in your schools/communities?

Sample Script for Agree to Mediate

Ainura (Mediator 1): *"Hello. First of all, I want to welcome you both to this mediation; thank you for coming."*

Rustam (Mediator 2): *"Welcome. My name is Rustam, and Ainura and I are here today to help you resolve the conflict between you."*

Ainura: *"What are your names, or how would you prefer that we address you?"*

Gulgan (Participant 1): *"You can call me Gulgan."*

Hamid (Participant 2): *"My name is Hamid."*

Rustam: *"Ok great, thanks. We'd like to explain a bit about how the mediation process works and what we'll be doing here today, and at the end if you have any questions, we'll be happy to answer them."*

Ainura: *"First we'll hear each of you tell your side of the story of what happened or what it is that is bothering you. We'll ask some questions to make sure that we understand you and then give you some more time to explain how you see things and how you feel. We'll try and help you listen to each other and then we'll see if we can come up with ideas for how to resolve the conflict. At the end, if we come up with a solution that is everyone feels is fair and that everyone agrees to, we can sign an agreement (or shake on it)."*

Rustam: *"The mediation can take up to an hour and a half. If anyone needs a break during the mediation, we can take one. If we reach the end of the time that we have today and we still haven't reached a resolution, we can always set up another mediation this week. Sometimes these things can take time."*

Ainura: *"It's important for us to make it clear that everything that you say here in this room stays between us. We won't tell our friends, our classmates, or our teachers about the things that you say here. The only exception is if someone is in danger of being hurt or hurting someone else – then we have to tell an adult. But you can feel safe here to share your feelings or to talk about things that we understand are difficult to talk about. We promise that we will listen, and we won't share what you say with anyone."*

Rustam: *"It's also important for us to tell you that our job is to help you understand each other better and hopefully to be able to come up with a solution that works for both of you. We're not here to judge you, or to decide who is right and who is wrong. As mediators we promise to try our hardest to remain neutral. We know that both of you have your own perspective and feelings about what happened, and we respect that."*

Ainura: *"That's about it. Does anyone have any questions about the process?"*

Gulgan: *"No, I understand."*

Hamid: *"Not really."*

Rustam: *"Great. Who would like to start by telling their side of the story*

Understanding Communication

Purpose:

To understand what communication is and why it is such an important component of conflict resolution and mediation.

Length: 1 hour

Number of Participants: 5 or more

Materials: flipchart, markers, Communication Handout, Communication Inhibitors Handout.

Procedure:

1. Read the "Communication" handout and the "Communication Inhibitors" together.

2. Discuss

   - Questions for Discussion

     o Why is communication so important in conflict resolution and in the mediation process?

     o What are some of the different ways that we communicate with each other?

     o Who do you know who you consider to be a good listener? What kinds of behaviors do they exhibit that make them good listeners?

     o What are some of the common "blocks" to effective communication?

     o Think about yourself. What most commonly blocks your own ability to listen to others?

     o Can you recognize any patterns in your own listening skills? What do you tend to do, or not to do, that either helps you communicate or inhibits your ability to do so effectively?

     o Why is it so important that mediators become good active listeners and understand the dynamics of effective communications?

Communication

"People fail to get along because they fear each other; they fear each other because they don't know each other; they don't know each other because they have not communicated with each other."

Martin Luther King

What is communication and why do we communicate with each other? The roots of the word communication point to action that is undertaken with the goal of sharing information or making something common to all those involved in the exchange of information. In other words, we could say that the goal of communication is to be understood, and to understand each other. This might sound like a simple task – how difficult can it be to engage in a process of exchanging information? In reality, communication is very complex. Communications can be verbal and non-verbal, and it is influenced by a wide range of factors including age, gender, race, socio-economic status, education level, and physical constraints.

Have you ever tried to resolve a conflict with a person who is unable to unwilling to listen? Whether this individual is distracted, reacting out of anger or fear, busy proving that they are right, blaming others, daydreaming, or planning their next response, it can be quite frustrating! Fortunately, most people have also had the good fortune of communicating with people who we consider to be good listeners. The truth is that listening is hard work! The term 'active listening' refers to a set of skills that includes bod language, listening, asking questions, and summarizing facts and feelings, and expressing empathy. In order to be a skilled active listener, one must be available for the committed to effective communication – someone who is able to reduce internal and external distractions, avoid making assumptions, and refrain from making unnecessary remarks or giving unasked for advice.

Communication is most effective when people are able to exchange information accurately about facts and feelings, and poor communication occurs when people are not able to accurately understand the facts and/or feeling being shared with them. Poor communication is often what lies beneath misunderstandings which then become unnecessary conflicts. There are many possible reasons why people are unable to communicate effectively, and many factors can "block" our ability to be effective communicators. Some of the more common communication blocks include poor body language, poor listening, using "you" statements and "loaded" words, and an unwillingness or inability to acknowledge differing perspectives.

As mediators and peacemakers, it is important that we know how to be active listeners. In conflict situations, it is our job to ask clarifying questions, summarize facts and feelings, and make sure that the speaker feels that he/she has been given a chance to be heard. Conflicts can often be resolved through active listening because throughout the process of listening to each other and truly hearing each other one or both of the parties realize that the conflict is simply the result of a misunderstanding. In cases where there is a true disagreement and a clash of needs, values, or resources, people who have been give an opportunity to have their perspective heard are more likely to be committed to achieving a win-win solution and are better equipped to eventually reach one because they are also able to understand and empathize with the other party.

Communication Inhibitors

Here is a list of some of the things that we all tend to do that make it difficult to listen to others. Can you think of situations in which either you or the person you were talking to fell into each of these patterns?

Interrupting
Judging
Criticizing
Changing the subject
Joking around
Offering advice
Laughing at others
Bringing up your own experiences
Distractions
Stereotyping
Making false assumptions

What is Active Listening?

Active listening is a communication skill that involves going beyond simply hearing the words that another person speaks but also seeking to understand the meaning and intent behind them. It requires being an active participant in the communication process.

Active listening techniques include:

- o   Being fully present in the conversation
- o   Showing interest by practicing good eye contact
- o   Noticing (and using) non-verbal cues
- o   Asking open-ended questions to encourage further responses.
- o   Paraphrasing and reflecting back what has been said.
- o   Listening to understand rather than to respond.
- o   Withholding judgment and advice

In communication, active listening is important because it keeps you engaged with your conversation partner in a positive way. It also makes the other person feel heard and valued. This skill is the foundation of a successful conversation in any setting—whether at work, at home, or in social situations.

When you practice active listening, you are fully engaged and immersed in what the other person is saying.

7 Active Listening Techniques

The word "active" implies that you are taking some type of action when listening to others. This involves the use of certain strategies or techniques. Here are seven active listening techniques to consider.

1. **Be Fully Present.**

   Active listening requires being fully present in the conversation. This enables you to concentrate on what is being said. Being present involves listening with all your senses (sight, sound, etc.) and giving your full attention to the speaker.

   To use this active listening technique effectively, put away your cell phone, ignore distractions, avoid daydreaming, and shut down your internal dialogue. Place your focus on your conversation partner and let everything else slip away.

2. **Pay Attention to Non-Verbal Cues**

   As much as 65% of a person's communication is unspoken. Paying attention to these nonverbal cues can tell you a lot about the person and what they are trying to say. If they talk fast, for instance, this could be a sign that they are nervous or anxious. If they talk slowly, they may be tired or trying to carefully choose their words.

   During active listening, your non-verbal behaviors are just as important. To show the person you're truly tuned in, use open, non-threatening body language. This involves not folding your arms, smiling while listening, leaning in, and nodding at key junctures.

   It can also be helpful to pay attention to your facial expressions when active listening so that you don't convey any type of negative response.

3. **Keep Good Eye Contact**

   When engaged in active listening, making eye contact is especially important. This tells the other person that you are present and listening to what they say. It also shows that you aren't distracted by anything else around you.

   At the same time, you don't want to use so much eye contact that the conversation feels weird. To keep this from happening, follow the 50/70 rule. This involves maintaining eye contact for 50% to 70% of the time spent listening, holding the contact for four to five seconds before briefly looking away.

4. Ask Open-Ended Questions

Asking "yes or no" questions often produces dead-end answers. This isn't helpful during active listening as it keeps the conversation from flowing. It also makes it difficult to truly listen to the other person because there isn't much you can gain from a short, non-descriptive response.

Instead, ask open-ended questions to show that you are interested in the conversation and the other person. Examples of open-ended questions you may use when active listening include:

- o Can you tell me a bit more about that?
- o What did you think about that?
- o What do you think is the best path moving forward?
- o How do you think you could have responded differently?

Open-ended questions encourage thoughtful, expansive responses, which is why they are often used by mental health therapists.

5. Reflect What You Hear

After the person has spoken, tell them what you heard. This active listening technique ensures that you've captured their thoughts, ideas, and/or emotions accurately. It also helps the other person feel validated and understood while keeping any potential miscommunications to a minimum.

One way to reflect what you've heard is to paraphrase. For example, you might say, "In other words, what you are saying is that you're frustrated" or "I'm hearing that you're frustrated about this situation." Summarize what you've heard and give the person the opportunity to say whether you've captured their meaning or intent.

If you'd like to better understand something the person has said, ask for clarification. But don't focus so much on insignificant details that you miss the big picture.

6. Be Patient

Patience is an important active listening technique because it allows the other person to speak without interruption. It also gives them the time to say what they are thinking without having you try to finish their sentences for them.

Being patient involves not trying to fill periods of silence with your own thoughts or stories. It also requires listening to understand, not to respond. That is, don't prepare a reply while the other person is still speaking. Also, don't change the subject too abruptly as this conveys boredom and impatience.

During active listening, you are there to act as a sounding board rather than to jump in with your own ideas and opinions about what is being said.

7. Withhold Judgment

Remaining neutral and non-judgmental in your responses enables the other person to feel comfortable with sharing their thoughts. It makes the conversation a safe zone where they can trust that they won't be shamed, criticized, blamed, or otherwise negatively received.

Ways to be less judgmental when listening include:

o   Expressing empathy for the person or their situation

o   Learning more about different people and cultures

o   Practicing acceptance of others

o   Recognizing when you may be judging the other person, then stopping those thoughts

Active Listening Example

What does active listening look like? Here is an example of a conversation in which several different active listening techniques are used.

Lisa: *"I'm sorry to dump this on you, but I had a fight with my sister, and we haven't spoken since. I'm upset and don't know who to talk to."*

Jodie: *"No problem! Tell me more about what happened."* (open-ended question)

Lisa: *"Well, we were arguing about what to do for our parents' anniversary. I'm still so angry."*

Jodie: *"Oh that's tough. You sound upset that you're not speaking because of it."* (Reflecting what was heard)

Lisa: *"Yes, she just makes me so angry. She assumed I would help her plan this elaborate party—I don't have time! It's like she couldn't see things from my perspective at all."*

Jodie: *"Wow, that's too bad. How did that make you feel?"* (Another open-ended question)

Lisa: *"Frustrated. Angry. Maybe a bit guilty that she had all these plans, and I was the one holding them back. Finally, I told her to do it without me. But that's not right, either."*

Jodie: *"Sounds complicated. I bet you need some time to sort out how you feel about it."* (Withholding judgment)

Lisa: *"Yes, I guess I do. Thanks for listening—I just needed to vent."*

Why Active Listening Is Important

Getting into the habit of active listening can have positive impacts in many key areas of your life. It can affect your relationships, your work, and your social interactions.

In Relationships

Active listening helps you better understand another person's point of view and respond with empathy. This is important in all types of healthy relationships, whether with a spouse, parent, child, another family member, or friend.

Being an active listener in your relationships involves recognizing that the conversation is more about the other person than about you. This is especially important when the other person is emotionally distressed.

Your ability to listen actively to a family member or friend who is going through a difficult time is a valuable communication skill. It helps keep you from offering opinions and solutions when the other person really just wants to be heard.

At Work

Active listening at work is particularly important if you are in a supervisory position or interact frequently with colleagues. It helps you understand problems and collaborate to develop solutions. It also showcases your patience, a valuable asset in the workplace.

In some cases, active listening while on the job can help improve workplace safety. For instance, if you are in the healthcare field, engaging in active listening can help reduce medical errors and prevent unintentional patient harm.

During Social Situations

Active listening techniques such as reflecting, asking open-ended questions, seeking clarification, and watching body language help you develop relationships when meeting new people. People who are active and empathic listeners are good at initiating and maintaining conversations.

Active listening helps others feel more emotionally supported. This can be beneficial when interacting with a person who has social anxiety. According to research, emotional support impacts the left dorsolateral prefrontal cortex of the brain, resulting in decreased feelings of distress for socially anxious individuals.

Ways to Improve Active Listening

We've all been in situations where our "listeners" were distracted or disinterested. Or maybe you want to improve your own active listening skills, so you don't do this to others.

Here are a few ways to be a better active listener yourself, or to encourage others to do the same:

- **Encourage your own curiosity.** The more curious you are about something, the easier it becomes to want to know more. This naturally causes you to ask more questions and to seek to understand, which are two of the core foundations of active listening in communication.

- **Find a topic that interests you both.** This works particularly well when engaging in small talk as you get to know one another. If you both have passion for the topic, it becomes easier to stay fully engaged in the conversation.

- **Practice your active listening skills.** Like with any skill, being good at active listening takes some practice. Be patient with yourself as you go through the learning process. Continuing to practice these skills may just inspire the person you're conversing with to do the same. By seeing you demonstrate active listening, they might become a better listener too.

- **Understanding when exiting the conversation is best.** If you're talking with another person and they are clearly uninterested in the conversation, it may be best to end that conversation respectfully. This can help keep you from feeling annoyed and unheard.

A Word from Verywell

Active listening is an important social skill that has value in many different settings. Practice its many techniques often and it will become second nature. You'll start to ask open-ended questions and reflect on what you've heard in your conversations without much (if any) thought.

If you find active listening techniques difficult, consider what might be getting in your way. Are you experiencing social anxiety during conversations, or do you struggle with attention? Getting help for these types of issues can help you improve your active listening skills, making you a better listener overall.

What is the purpose of active listening?

Active listening helps you build trust and understand other people's situations and feelings. In turn, this empowers you to offer support and empathy. Unlike critical listening, active listening seeks to understand rather than reply. The goal is for the other person to be heard, validated, and inspired to solve their problems.

What are the 3 A's of active listening?

The three A's of active listening are attention, attitude, and adjustment. Attention entails being fully tuned in to the speaker's words and gestures. The proper attitude is one of positivity and open-mindedness. Adjustment is the ability to change your gestures, body language, and reactions as the speaker's story unfolds.

Which active listening technique involves empathy?

Reflection is an active listening technique that demonstrates that you understand and empathize with the person's feelings. In mirroring and summarizing what they've said, they feel heard and understood.

How can I improve my active listening skills?

There are numerous ways to improve your active listening skills. One is to watch skilled interviewers on talk and news shows. Another is to research active listening techniques online and try them often in your everyday conversations, noting the speakers' reactions and looking for areas that need improvement.

The Art of Forgiving

As individuals go through life, they must find the tools that will work for them. As it is written in Matthew 25; 14 – 26, God gave three disciples talents. He gave the one disciple one talent, the second disciple two talents, and the third disciple, three talents.

The first one buried his talent, the second doubled his and the third doubled his. The two disciples that doubled their talents was rewarded by God and the one that buried this talent was admonished by God.

In essence, God will reward you if you work hard and develop the talent, he gives you. Just to illustrate my point, everyone cannot play football, baseball, soccer, tennis, hockey, as well as others. Some can sing, dance, and write better than others. Others become doctors, lawyers, technologists, computer specialists, electricians, machinists, dentists, etc. It is your responsibility to use the talents that God has give you.

I believe that God gave me the talent to be a problem solver in all areas, negotiator, mediator, arbitrator, and fact finder. However, I had to recognize what my talents were and act on them. After I acknowledged my talents, there were some issues that I had to deal with in order to be successful as a problem solver.

I quickly learned that there were six companions that I had to learn to live with in order to expand upon my God given talents.

1. I had to learn to live with (myself) by being able to show compassion for others, apologize if I offended someone and be able to allow for mistakes and forgive others. I had to be honest with myself and seriously practice self-examination in order to understand who I am. What were my goals in life, how do I get to where I want to go? I further had to learn how to deal with difficult people.

2. I had to learn to live with (others): by understanding the importance of friendship, relationships, loyalty, and being able to exchange positions with others and developing good listening skills. Treat others the way you want to be treated and be respectful at all times.

3. I had to learn to live with challenges: by learning that every single day, there are going to be different challenges at home, work, and the community.

4. I had to learn to live with acknowledge (change) and become a change agent, because 85% to 90% of the changes made are good. Change is inevitable and waits on no one.

5. I had to learn to live with (choices) because if an individual makes bad choices early in life, it could impact them for the rest of their life.

6. I had to learn to live with (conflict) because I learned that conflict is something we simply cannot avoid. The focus has to be on how to resolve conflict.

After learning and practicing the above six companions, I was equipped to tackle real life issues which prepared me for successfully navigating the system to become one of the most successful negotiators, mediator, and arbitrator in the nation.

In addition, I had to learn the importance and power of forgiveness. I had to ask myself the rhetorical question, are there limits to forgiving? Is there something that individuals could do to you that would prohibit you from ever forgiving them? Suppose someone harmed you, your wife, or other family members physically or emotionally, could you forgive them, or would you typically want to harm them as they have harmed you?

Keep in mind that forgiveness is not some kind of miracle cure that can solve all of the problems of your life. However, it is a foundational issue we must deal with. When we have anger and bitterness stored up inside of us, we must learn to forgive. We may even need to forgive over and over again. There is no escape from living in a sinful world. When sinners live together, they will sooner or later (probably sooner) do things that irritate, upset, and hurt others. Forgiveness makes it possible for irritation to be overlooked and deep hurt healed.

The Bible tells us that we should forgive seven times seventy. It goes further and insists that you don't count the number of times you forgive someone. In fact, forgiveness is not impossible, and it helps the forgiver sometimes as much helps the individual who did the harm. Forgiveness is unlimited and very difficult, but not impossible.

Many of us have lived far too long with unresolved hurts going back many years. We have been angry and bitter all that time in many instances over a simple misunderstanding. The hidden torturers have done their work. No wonder many marriages fail and both parties are continuously unhappy. No wonder divorce and legal separations seem like a good alternative. No wonder we make a decision to shut a friend or coworker out of our lives over simple misunderstandings or seek revenge by participating in gun violence through mass shootings.

Where Does Forgiving Start?

- Perhaps forgiving from your heart means writing a letter of forgiveness to the individual who hurt you. (DON'T MAIL IT)

- Perhaps it means confessing to a friend that you are struggling with issues of forgiveness.

- Perhaps it means listing the other person's offenses one by one and writing over them "forgiven" and then offering the list to God in prayer.

- If you can come to terms and are willing to forgive another person, there is no requirement to tell that person that you forgave them. You have to forgive them in your heart.

After you have done your part by forgiving another individual, there are instances where both parties really want to restore their relationship but simply do not have an avenue to reconnect. Therefore, there are seven steps that can be used to rebuild a relationship through the art of communication and willingness to forgive. They are as follows:

- Ask the individual(s) if they are willing to discuss the issues that caused the conflict. If they agree, ask if it would be appropriate to include a third party to assist you. A mutual friend that you both trust could act as a mediator if needed.

- Start the conversation by saying something nice about the opposing party. For example, recall some positive things that you have done together prior to the dispute. Acknowledge a past and positive relationship.

- Prior to the meeting, instead of thinking about who was at fault, only focus on what it will take to resolve the matter. Do not use the rear-view mirror tactics because you will only be able to see behind you. Use the windshield approach because you can see more into the future. If you use the rear-view mirror, it will prohibit you from solving your conflict.

- Tell the person what is on your mind. Only talk about their behavior and how it affects you. Do not be accusatory finger pointing, degrading and empathy.

- Give the individual an opportunity to respond and listen with sympathy and empathy.

- Ask for a change in behavior.

- Thank the person for their time and agreeing to meet. If necessary, schedule a follow up meeting.

Generally speaking, if individuals really want to resolve the matter, all they need to do is follow the above steps in the order they are listed. If you skip any one, it will hamper the process.

The Consequences of Refusing to Forgive

Before I share with you the consequences of the failure to forgive, I decided to share with you the greatest act of forgiveness that I have ever witnessed. It involved my brother Cozy Brown who owns a restaurant in Whistler, Alabama.

On June 16, 2016, he was robbed by a 20-year-old young man who brutally beat him and shot him. Fortunately, the bullet did not hit any of his vital organs, if so, he possibly could have died. He was hospitalized for several days before he returned to work. Upon returning to work, he was contacted by the District Attorney regarding this matter. My brother informed the District Attorney that he did not want to press any charges against the young man and that he had already forgiven him. The young man avoided the police for several weeks and was finally arrested. Several months later, the judge asked him what he would like to see happen to this young man, Cozy asked the judge to give the young man to him and he would give him a job and counsel him because God spared his life for him to do something good.

That was the greatest act of forgiveness I ever witnessed because most individuals would have pressed charges against the young man and demanded that he be jailed for an extended period of time.

On the other hand, there are thousands of instances where individuals hold grudges for your and refuse to forgive others for what I termed "simple misunderstanding." I have observed numerous individuals who have shared with me the cruelest statement I have ever witnessed. They informed me that they haven't seen or spoken to their mother, father, sister, or brother for years. In some instances, it could be justified, but in my opinion, it is inconceivable to me that individuals are able to get so angry with their immediate family that they avoid talking to them for years.

I contend that in some instances, time heals wounds and individuals should be able to forgive their family members for their own benefit. Once you are born into a family, regardless of what they do, you cannot divorce them. No matter what you say or do, that still is your mother, father, sister, or brother.

What really astonish me is this happens with individuals who call themselves Christians. They will go to church every Sunday, serve on various boards in the church, attend Bible study and go to the altar and pray. They will pray for themselves and ask God to forgive them for their sins while they are unwilling to forgive a family member for a simple misunderstanding. How can God forgive you when you are unwilling to forgive others? I remind individuals that we are all guilty of saying something; we wish we could roll back. However, even when we say something that we know is inflammatory and deeply offends another person, in most instances, we are unwilling to even apologize or forgive the person that you assume offended you. In our hearts we are unwilling to practice the art of forgiving.

ANGER MANAGEMENT

Of all the human emotional feelings society experiences daily, anger is the most powerful and poorly handled feeling. Although anger is considered to be a healthy normal human emotion. It varies in intensity from mild irritation to intense fury and rage. It has the ability to take control and become destructive, leading to problems in your work and personal life as well as jeopardizing the quality of your life.

Anger can be a friend or an enemy depending on the way in which you choose to express it. Responding aggressively is the natural way to express anger. It is a natural adaptive response to threats. Anger inspires powerful often-aggressive feelings and behaviors that allow us to fight and to defend ourselves when attacked. Therefore, one can say that anger is necessary for survival. Feelings of anger are normal, something experienced by everyone, and a powerful feeling that one can learn to manage.

People use a variety of both conscious and unconscious processes to deal with their angry feelings. You cannot change, avoid, or get rid of the things or the people that enrage you. However, you can learn to control your reactions to anger. Knowing how to recognize and express it appropriately can help you reach your goals, solve problems, handle emergencies effectively, and protect your health. The inability to recognize and understand one's anger can lead to a variety of personal difficulties. Not until you learn to choose your attitudes will you have the power and freedom to be your own person, capable of determining and achieving your goals and dreams. It is not easy to change negative attitudes. It takes time and practice. When you act instead of reacting, the joy and success experienced when you see an opportunity instead of a problem is the greatest gift you can give yourself.

The object of the anger management program is to reduce both your emotional feelings and the physiological arousal caused by anger. The anger management program designed will help to:

Empower individuals to obtain understanding of how they perceive and respond to events around them.

- Learn to transform negative attitudes into positive ones.

- Increase understanding of the bodies response to anger.

- Develop effective techniques to manage anger.

- Increase self-awareness and affirm strengths, talents, and abilities.

- Overcome self-imposed limitations, fears, and doubts.

- Develop effective listening and communication skills.

- Improve relationships and increase empathy and respect for others.

- Achieve new levels of performance through goal-setting techniques.

- Learn practical and effective approaches to problem solving.

Six Level Used in Communicating Emotions

1. Small talk – Casual, passing conversation that usually means nothing. When you do this, you use the cliches such as "How are things going?" or "What have you been doing?" This level is just casual passing communication that means nothing except it is better than embarrassing silence.

2. Talk about things and people – Usual luncheon or break conversation. Events, people, and happenings are related, but you tell little about yourself—only what you have been doing rather than who you are.

3. Your reveal your opinions, thoughts, and ideas – Inner thoughts, risking, criticism, or disagreement. At the first indication of rejection, you may go back to small talk or talking about things/people.

4. Your emotions talk – Due to wounds or hurt, your emotions take over and do the talking. You may express anger, jealousy, or hostility saying things you regret later. Alternately, in some instances, you may be carried away by positive emotions –excitement, attraction, or enthusiasm.

5. You talk about the way you feel and who you are – Talking emotions honestly and courageously. Doubts, fears, anger, hopes, joys, feelings about yourself are all voices. Growth results as you begin to know yourself and help others get to know themselves.

6. Peak communications – Rare moments when you are perfectly in tune with another communicating with understanding, depth, and emotional satisfaction.

    • When you described your reactions to the examples in the previous project, at what level of communication were they?

    • How do you attempt to control or manage emotions? What are the results? All people are emotional…although some seem to experience emotions more intensely than most. How do you see yourself? How has your life been influenced by emotions?

Other Activities:

    • Sharing your emotions – Partner activity based on a list of emotions provided to each participant.

    • Emotional Positions and Taking Charge of your emotions:

        – I will act the way I feel, you're going to act the way I feel; I can't help the way I feel, but I can help the way I think and act.

            • Removing Roadblocks

            • Dealing with Anger

            • Expressing Anger

            • Strategies to Keep Anger at Bay

Dealing with Emotions

Purpose:

- To examine and understand the role that emotions play in conflict.

- To learn concrete steps for dealing with difficult emotions such as anger.

Length: 1 hour

Number of Participants: 6 or more

Materials: Handout "Steps to Dealing with Emotions"

Procedure:

1. Provide the participants with the handout "Steps to Dealing with Emotions."

2. Read the handout together with the participants.

3. Discuss the role that emotions play in our day-to-day lives and how they surface during conflicts. Go over the steps for dealing with difficult emotions and talk about each one.

4. Ask the participants to write/draw/talk about a specific experience they have had in which they were dealing with a difficult emotion, going through the steps one by one.

Steps to Dealing with Emotions

Everyone has emotions. The following steps are a helpful way to deal with emotions that you want to change:

1. **Name the emotion:** Go beyond simple descriptors like mad, sad, happy to think more deeply about what you are feeling and why.

2. **Claim the emotion:** Recognize that the emotion is your own. No one gave it to you but it is yours and it represents how you feel. Even if the emotion isn't the best response to the situation, it is your response to the situation.

3. **Tame the emotion:** Take a step that works for you, such as taking 3 deep breaths or swaying the alphabet to yourself silently to step away from the intensity of the feeling.

4. **Reframe the emotion:** Ask yourself under what conditions you've felt this same emotion in the past. What are the factors that typically lead up to this emotion.

5. **Aim the emotion:** Now that you're better understood the emotion, ask what you're going to do to change it. Can you reframe your thinking so that those same conditions do not create this same emotion? Do you need to speak with someone else who is often involved when you feel this emotion? Create a plan and stick to it.

THREE RESPONSES TO ANGER

1. Ignoring/Denial/Suppression

Acting as though nothing has happened.

2. Aggression

Attacking the person in a verbal, non-verbal or physical way. Giving someone the cold shoulder or hurling insults back are two examples of aggressive behavior.

3. Assertiveness

Letting the person know how you feel without hurting the person in return.

VIOLENCE

Anything one does to knowingly harm another individual; be it psychologically, mentally, verbally, or physically is an act of violence.

FIVE STEPS TO MANAGING ANGER

1. **Recognize your anger**

   - Pay attention

   - Notice your feelings

   - Research your anger

2. **Cool down**

   - Leave the situation

   - Work it off

   - Let it out

   - Relax

3. **Figure it out**

   - Understand your feelings.

   - Decide what you want to see changed.

4. **Talk about it**

   - Set some ground rules.

   - Remember that how you say something is as important as what you say.

- Say what you need.

- Compromise

5. Protect yourself

- Stay safe.

- Put yourself in the other person's shoes

- Find options.

- Be willing to apologize.

Engaging in Productive Dialogues

To dialogue means to:

- Inquire

- Learn

- Offer thoughts

- Discover shared vision

- Discover common meaning

- Bring together a whole system's view

- Investigate assumptions/beliefs

- To explore what it mean to think and lean as a collective

Five Steps to Engage in Productive Dialogue

1. Show up and be fully present

- Use personal power in appropriate ways

- Show honor and respect

- Exhibit careful communication

2. Pay Attention

- Acknowledge our own and other's assumptions

- Suspend those assumptions

- Acknowledge others' skills, opinions, qualities and impact

3. Tell the truth

- Without blame/judgment

- Personal vision

4. Be open-minded

- Be open to outcome(s), not attached to outcome(s)

5. Creativity

- Create a new mind, a new learning which is owned by the group

Communication Realities

- You cannot **NOT** communicate.

- Whenever contact occurs, communication occurs

- Meaning cannot be transferred from one mind to another... only **WORDS** can.

- **ALL** communications are received...70% to 90% are screened or changed by receiver.

Effective Communication

- Give speakers your full attention

- Ask questions for clarity

- Summarize and paraphrase for understanding

- Tune into words, feelings, body language

Managing Change

- Change, whether anticipated or unanticipated, can be difficult!

- **_Change_** is an event that is situational and external to us. Something stops and something starts.

- **_Transition_** is the gradual, psychological reorientation process that happens inside of us as we adapt to external change.

Three Phases of Transition Process

1. **ENDINGS** – When we disengage from the old way of doing things and let go of who we were in that situation.

2. **NEUTRAL ZONE** – When we find ourselves in a confusing in-between state, when we are not who and where we were, but not yet who we will be and where we are going.

3. **NEW BEGINNINGS** – When we grow familiar with and accept (but not necessarily like) the new reality change brings.

AM I READY?

People are said to resist change, but more often it is the transition they resist. People do not resist change; they resist the disruption that change causes in their expectations.

Building Bridges to Understanding

As the dramatic shift to a highly diverse workforce continues, organizations, large and small, know they must do a better job of help all workers understand, accept, and capitalize on differences. They know the cultural backgrounds and experience of diverse employees, and customers can deeply enrich the organization, making it more innovative and globally competitive. Changes in employment practice require the rapid adjustment of employers and employees. Gives the reality of individual uniqueness in the workplace, the Building Bridges to Understanding – Relationship by Objective concept is designed to access the perceptions, values, and behaviors we embrace in work groups and individual work settings.

After having in-depth dialogue with the participants, it is apparent to our company that there are areas that will benefit from our services due to the following reasons. During our dialogue, it will be revealed that there are several areas of concern that requires immediate assistance and attention; we believe that the most pressing need is conflict resolution training and the implementation of our System Navigation process due to the issues and concern that surfaced during our dialogue.

Therefore Hez Brown & Associates, LLC is proposing the following concept to address the training and educational needs of: Supervisors, professional and non-professional staff, mid- and executive level staff, and community.

Generally speaking, experience has taught us that in developing programs for corporations, educational and other institutions, there are no silver bullets that cover all situations, nor is there one program that fits every situation. That is why it is important for the individuals and departments that agree to participate to be involved in the planning and preparatory process. Hez Brown & Associates involve the participants by conducting a needs and assessment analysis by meeting with a percentage of staff and asking them all the same questions. For example:

- What are the major problems they face daily at home, at work, and the community?

- What are some of the issues that need to be addressed to make your job easier?

- How would you rate the morale of your co-workers?

- Are there any specific issues that need immediate attention?

Then the staff is asked to explain specifically how they would address these problems. The essence of this process is that it is very easy to point out a problem, but it takes skill and understanding to solve a problem. The program will then be designed to address the issues that surface during the needs and assessment process and other concerns as appropriate.

We further recommend that the first stop after the Need assessment would be the implementation of the Building Bridges for a Better Understanding – Relationship by Objective Process – RBO. Each participant will be required to complete an online DISC profile prior to the initial session. In addition, participants are encouraged to be prepared to work in small groups and define the problems and it will be their responsibility to seek rational and doable solutions to the problems.

The RBO is an issue-oriented approach used to redesign management-employee, co-workers and community relationships. It is an in-depth, conflict resolution process that brings parties together to analyze their current relationship/issues: reach agreement on the issues and jointly develop common objectives to build more productive relationships. The parties also agree on an action plan and assign specific responsibilities to implement and achieve the objectives that they have set for their relationship.

RBO requires the total commitment, support and involvement of key officials and employees to succeed. The effort all individuals exercise in achieving the objectives they set for their improved relationships is also critical. The RBO will be successful only if representatives at all levels acknowledge that they have a need for and are willing to accept assistance in resolving problems of mutual concern.

RBO requires that participants meet offsite for up to three days, in intensive RBO sessions facilitated by a team of Hez Brown & Associates facilitators. During the RBO process, individuals perform specific tasks in small group settings. In the small groups, individuals identify problems they face on a day to day basis. A thorough and candid discussion is held to air all problems and to reach a mutual understanding of the issues. Then the participants jointly develop a list of mutual objectives to overcome their problems. Objectives are normally grouped under the following categories:

1. Attitudes and Practices

2. Communication'

3. Health and safety

4. Management-employees relations

5. Operations

6. Practices and Procedures

7. Training

Participants are encouraged to use creative problem-solving tools to develop and recommend action steps and develop a plan to meet the objectives. The discussions will be based on realistic and practical implementation steps.

The RBO process is designed to eliminate factors that cause breakdowns in communication, relationships and solve long term issues between co-workers, managers, and supervisors. RBO focuses on intergroup team building, intragroup image clarification and diagnosis, confrontation meetings, coaching and other developmental approaches. The program consists of five phases:

1. Problem solving and goal setting.

2. Action planning and programming

3. Implementation of plans and programs

4. Periodic review and evaluation of programs toward goal accomplishments.

5. In depth training on communication skills, managing change, conflict management, team building, anger management, leadership, and problem-solving skills.

Phases 1, 4, and 5 take place at a neutral off-site location for three intensive days. 20 to 30 members of the management and staff attend sessions with facilitators supplied by Hez Brown & Associates. Separate and joint sessions are held until mutual problems and goal statements are clarified covering such topics as communication, attitudes including supervisor and staff issues. Since its inception, the RBO process has had positive results, including improved stability in the party's relationships, less personal grievances, improved production and improved morale and smoother day to day operation.

The evaluation process will be conducted with 45 day follow up and an additional 45-day evaluation until the project is completed. At the conclusion of the project is completed. At the conclusion of the project, Hez Brown & Associates will provide the institution with a written report outlining the strengths and weaknesses of the process.

Pointers About Dealing with People

1. **People differ greatly.** Differences in physical appearances are easy to see but differences in psychological make-up are probably greater and more important.

2. **Behavior is emotional as well as logical.** People do things not only because they are sensible but also because of the way they feel.

3. **To change a person's attitude** – one must first find how he feels and then show time how the change will benefit him personally.

4. **The atmosphere for change in attitudes** must include respect

for the right of individual opinions, room in which to save face, and each must feel that his democratic rights are fully protected.

5. **Be a good listener.** Listen patiently to the other. Find out what is really the basis for his opinion. Show real interest.

6. **Stick to the point.** Have your facts in order and ready for a prompt presentation.

7. **Use pauses in your talk.** Halt occasionally so that your points will sink in.

8. **Easy does it.** When one pounds the table, his brain works less. Keep cool but do not freeze —few can think their best if too hot or too cold.

9. **Use a positive friendly approach.** Your response will be the same — a soft answer turns away wrath. Avoid an aggressive or defensive attitude.

10. **Keep an open mind. Be loose.** Listen for and accept new facts. Be willing to graciously admit error and accept confirmation in one's position.

Roadblock to Communication

ORDERING: "You must…"

"You have to…"

"You will…"

THREATENING: "If you don't, then…"

"You had better or else…"

PREACHING: "It is your duty to…"

"You should…"

"You must…"

LECTURING: "Here is why you are wrong…"

"Do you realize…"

PROVIDING ANSWERS: "What I would do is…"

"It you be best for you…"

JUDGING: "You are bad…lazy!"

"Your hair is too long…"

EXCUSING: "You'll feel better…"

"It's not so bad…"

DIAGNOSING: "You're just trying to get attention…"

"I know what you need…"

PRYING: "Why?"

"What?"

"How?"

"When?"

For Open Communication and Better Cooperation

Six most important words you can use:

"I was wrong – I am sorry."

Five most important words:

"You did a good job."

Four most important words:

"What do you think?"

Three most important words:

"Can I help?"

Two most important words:

"Thank you."

One most important word:

"You!"

Understanding Diversity

The extent to which an individual comprehends how others feel and why they behave as they do.

Awareness

With awareness, we start to see that our personal reality may not be the only reality. Awareness helps us apply our knowledge and information base to how it feels to interact with people different from ourselves. It clarifies who we are in comparison to other people's perceptions of us. This gives us a basis for contrasting our cultural viewpoint with that of another person and understanding that, because of culture, people may see the same situation differently.

Empathy

Empathy shows one's ability to make connections with others on an emotional level. People who are empathic and aware can comprehend the emotions others are experiencing. They tend to recognize the reasons for the points of view held by people from diverse backgrounds. Empathy allows us to put ourselves in other people's shoes, trying to perceive how it feels to "walk their way." It makes us more flexible and less resistant, allowing us to become more sensitive to differences among individuals.

Suggestions for Improving Your Understanding of Diverse Groups:

1. Attend a cultural event that you've never experienced in the past. Reflect on how you feel about being there. Try to become more aware of the impact and sensations that the experience has on you.

2. Setting aside your personal biases, observe an individual who appears to be part of the culture at this event and think about how that person feels about the activity. How different do you believe his/her experience is from you own?

3. After the event, discuss how you felt about being there with a person who is part of another ethnic, racial, religious or lifestyle group.

Acceptance

The extent to which an individual respects and values diverse characteristics and behaviors of others.

Tolerance

Tolerance is a component of accepting others who are different from oneself. With increased tolerance an individual is open and relaxed when interacting with others. He/she is able to accept the notion that all people be allowed to reflect their background and culture in their behavior. Tolerance grants others the same freedom of behavior and style that we expect for ourselves.

Respect

Respect goes beyond simply "putting up" with others' differences. With respect, we are able to grant full regard to people without compromise, based totally on the qualities appropriate to the task at hand. One's views of other people are not blemished or tarnished by negative cultural or racial characterizations. Ultimate respect is seeing value in having people base their contributions on their background and culture. When encouraged, respect creates change through trust.

Suggestions for Improving Your Acceptance of Diverse Groups:

1. Reflect on those feelings which, in the past, have prevented you from associating with someone from a particular group.

2. Think about and write down some of your fears/concerns about a cultural group. From 1 (the least likely) to 5 (most likely), what are the chances that each fear/concern might be realized? Write down the appropriate number for each response.

3. Create an opportunity to interact with someone from a group with whom you've been fearful of being uncomfortable about having close contact.

Behavior

The extent to which an individual is able to interact effectively with others different from herself/himself.

Self-Awareness

With self-awareness one understands his/her values, motives, and personal beliefs. At this level, one is conscious of personal strengths and weaknesses, and is sensitive to the effect he/she has on others. We develop the skills necessary to adjust our behavior while still maintaining our identity, values, and beliefs. Knowing who we are and how we impact other people helps us choose appropriate behavior.

Interpersonal Skills

A skillful person can manage situations and successfully interact with people who may be different from himself/herself. At this point, we are able to modify our behavior to meet the needs of a situation. Effective interpersonal skills reflect an ability to be flexible in reacting to the ideas and opinions of others. It shows them respect and trust through cooperation, attentiveness, and friendliness. This, in turn, results in more harmonious relationships and increased productivity.

Suggestions for Improving Your Behavior with Diverse Groups:

1. Ask for in-depth feedback from someone who knows you about his/her perception of your ability to interact with people from diverse backgrounds. Constructively discuss any differences in you point of view.

2. Select two to three items from his/her feedback list where you can improve. Think about ways to do so and create an action plan for change.

3. Seek an opportunity to interact with a group where you are the only representative from your culture. First attempt to become a member of the group then an active participant, while, at the same time, maintaining your own identity.

Considerations for Interaction with Other Cultures:

Social Space

Different cultures have different average distances at which people stand to talk to each other. Of course, this varies according to the circumstances and the relationships of the people. What is the distance at which you feel most comfortable speaking to another person? How do you feel when someone stands too close to you? Too far? About how far is that?

Touching

Where, how and how often people touch each other while conversing is often determined by cultural norms. In many cultures, some touching is acceptable between people of the same gender, but not between males and females, even husbands and wives, if they are in public. Males holding hands has no connotation except friendship in many countries. How do youfeel when someone touches your arm or hand? How weel do you need to know a person in order for you to feel comfortable when he or she taps you casually? Have you ever tapped a person casually and had him or her react strongly? Might culture have been a factor? How do you react to same-sex touching?

Volume of Voice

In some cultures, children are taught that a soft voice is polite, a loud voice, rude. In other cultures, a loud voice indicates strength of conviction, passion in one's belief. What sounds right to you? How do you feel when you perceive that someone is yelling at you? How about when someone is speaking softer than you are used to? What assumptions do you make about someone who speaks softly in a meeting? How about loudly?

Eye Contact

In some cultures, eye contact is perceived as an integral part of human contact. In others, it is seen as disrespectful, rude, aggressive, or flirtatious. Lack of eye contact, on the other hand, can be perceived as lack of attention by some, or as showing lack of interest, low self-esteem, or dishonesty. How do you feel when someone looks right at you throughout a conversation? Does it make you feel uncomfortable, or does it make you feel listened to? How about when someone doesn't look at you as much as you are accustomed to?

Gestures

Pointing with a finger is considered very rude in some cultures. Pointing with a foot is considered rude in others. In other cultures, pointing is a mainstay of everyday human interaction. What are gestures that you consider rude? Are they the same for the person sitting next to you?

Timing of Verbal Exchanges and Silence

In some cultures, when conversing, normal behavior is an immediate response to every exchange. Silence is perceived as disinterest or lack of attention and makes some people uncomfortable. However, in other cultures, people anticipate silence before a response. In this case, a response said too quickly can indicate a lack of proper thought to what the other person said. What is not said may be more important in the exchange than what is said. How do you feel when people respond to you quickly? Do you feel that they have not thought enough about what you said; do you feel that they are responding properly? How about when someone takes some time before responding? Does that indicate a well-thought-out response to you? Do you interpret a slow response as an indication that the person has limited intelligence?

Smiles

Smiles in some cultures are commonly used to cover anger, embarrassment or upset. Smiles in other cultures express "thank you" or "I'm sorry." In some cultures, a smile is considered flirtatious., a "come on." How do you perceive smiles? Do you smile at people in public, or is your smile reserved for family and friends? How do you feel when you smile at someone, and he or she doesn't smile back What does that mean to you?

Diversity Defined

What diversity is:

Diversity is recognizing, appreciating, valuing, and utilizing the unique talents and contributions of all individuals.

Diversity means different or varied. Diversity is the mosaic of people who bring a variety of backgrounds, styles, perspectives, values, and beliefs as assets to the groups and organizations with which they interact.

Prejudice

A set of attitudes, opinions, feelings, perceptions, or assumptions generalized about an individual or a particular group or groups.

These are formed:

- Without having information;
- In disregard of facts; or
- Based on past experiences (either negative or positive).

Discrimination:

Prejudice + Action

Mistreatment, injustice, or differential treatment based on prejudice/bias. When we act on our prejudices, we engage in discrimination.

Oppression

The systematic mistreatment of a group by an individual, a group or an institution that has access to "power."

The mistreatment may be emotional, verbal, mental, physical, economic, social and/or political.

Prejudice + Behavior = Discrimination

Discrimination + Power = Oppression

Collusion

Blatant bias is becoming a rarity in the contemporary workplace. Most people have enough common sense not to publicly violate the law. However, a much more common (and often unconscious) form of exclusion occurs regularly – collusion. Collusion is defined as:

Cooperation with others, knowingly or unknowingly, to reinforce stereotypical attitudes, prevailing behaviors, and norms.

Loden & Rosener, Workforce America! - 1991

Collusion is common because of the way we are socialized as children. We all had to modify our own behavior to "fit in" to expectations of parents, teachers, friends, and society. We become accustomed to ignoring our true opinions and needs as a way of increasing our sense of belonging and reducing the risk of being an "outsider." As adults, we are now able to make our own decisions about what we do and do not believe, and how to act on those decisions, rather than continuing the habit of "fitting in." There are three types of collusion: silence, denial, and active cooperation.

Silence

Silence is the most common form of collusion. By saying nothing when people tell jokes, exclude other, or exhibit other inappropriate behavior, we reinforce the "status quo." This is one reason for having diversity training and education – so that people will feel freer to speak up.

Denial

Denial sounds like a passive form of collusion, but it is actually the active stance that "no inequality exists here." After reading the statistics, or even looking at U.S. society in general, it is difficult to support the opinion that any organization is totally free of discrimination. Usually,

94

people who participate in collusion by denial are either avoiding the painful prospect that inequality exists, or they feel they have something to lose by acknowledging it.

Active Cooperation

Active cooperation can take several forms, some of which can be very subtle. Laughing at inappropriate jokes is active cooperation. Agreeing that "so and so just got that promotion because they filled a quota" is active cooperation. Participating in exclusionary networking activities (golf, dinners, etc.) is active cooperation.

The Cold Within

Six humans trapped by happenstance
In black and bitter cold
Each one possessed a stick of wood
Or so the story's told

Their dying fire in need of logs
The first woman held hers back
For the faces around the fire
She noticed one of them was black.

The next man looking cross the way
Saw one not of his church,
And couldn't bring himself to give
The first his stick of birch.

The third one sat in tattered clothes
He gave his coat a hitch,
Why should his log be put to use
To warm the idle rich?

The rich man just sat back and thought
Of the wealth he had in store,
And how to keep what he had earned
From the lazy, shiftless poor.

The black man's face bespoke revenge
As the fire passed from his sight
For all he saw in his stick of wood
Was a chance to spite the white.

And the last man of this forlorn group
Did naught except for gain,
Giving only to those who gave
Was how he played the game.

The logs held tight in death's still hands
Was proof of human sin,
They didn't die from the cold without
They died from the cold within.

Author Unknown

Diversity Definitions and Terms

Ableism

Ableism is prejudice and/or discrimination against people with mental and/or physical disabilities.

Affirmative Action

Affirmative action was created to ensure that employers took positive steps to attract, promote, and retain women and minorities if they were underrepresented in the company's workforce. This legislation was forced onto employers and came to be viewed as "quota filling." While affirmative action was a necessary step, it created an 'us versus them' mentality.

Ageism

Ageism is prejudice and/or discrimination against people because of their age.

American with Disabilities Act

The American with Disabilities Act, passed in 1989, requires employers to make "reasonable accommodations" in employing people with job-related limitations. The main impact is on selection and job descriptions in employment, and in modifying facilities for buildings and retail outlets. This law applies to 43 million people, including those with HIV and AIDS, as well as many other people.

Anti-bias

Anti-bias is an active commitment to challenging prejudice, stereotyping and all forms of discrimination.

Anti-Semitism

Anti-Semitism is prejudice and/or discrimination against Jews. Anti-Semitism can be based on hatred toward Jews because of their religious beliefs and/or their group membership (ethnicity).

Backlash

Backlash occurs when people feel they have something to lose by valuing diversity. Programs such as "quota filling" and diversity efforts that blame certain groups for past injustices, create a 'win lose' situation in which the targeted group resists and can even sabotage the effort.

Bias

Bias is an inclination or preference either for or against an individual or group that interferes with impartial judgment.

Bigotry

Bigotry is an unreasonable or irrational attachment to negative stereotypes and prejudices.

Classism

Classism is prejudice and/or discrimination against people because of their real or perceived economic status.

Collusion

Collusion is cooperation with others, knowingly or unknowingly, to reinforce stereotypical attitudes, prevailing behaviors, and norms.

Culture

Culture is the patterns of daily life learned consciously and unconsciously by a group of people. These patterns can be seen in language, governing practices, arts, customs, holiday celebrations, food, religion, dating rituals and clothing, to name a few examples.

Discrimination

Discrimination is the denial of justice and fair treatment by both individuals and institutions in many arenas, including employment, education, housing, banking, and political rights. Discrimination is an action that can follow prejudicial thinking.

Diversity

Diversity means different or varied. Diversity is the mosaic of people who bring a variety of backgrounds, styles, perspectives, values, and beliefs as assets to the groups and organizations with which they interact.

Equal Employment Opportunity (EEO)

Equal Employment Opportunity legislation was enacted to prohibit discrimination on the basis of "race," color, religion, gender, national origin, age, (dis)ability, or veteran status. It has since been updated to include sexual orientation. EEO attempted to provide applicants and employees with equitable treatment in an organization's human resources practices, including recruitment, hiring, training, compensation, and promotion.

Ethnocentrism

Ethnocentrism is the belief that one's group is inherently superior to all others.

Gender

Gender refers to whether a person is male or female. It is preferable to the term "sex" which can have other meanings. It is not related to sexual orientation (see that definition).

Heterosexism

Heterosexism is a system of attitudes, behaviors, cultural norms & institutional practices that denies, stigmatizes, and denigrates people who are gay, lesbian, or bisexual in U.S. society. Heterosexism is the default assumption that all people are heterosexual. Homophobia is the irrational fear of people who are believed to be gay, lesbian, or bisexual. Discrimination against people who are or who are perceived to be lesbian, gay, or bisexual are considered to be homophobic acts.

Multicultural

Multicultural means many or multiple culture. The United States is multicultural because its population consists of people from many different cultures.

Oppression

Oppression is the systematic mistreat of a group by an individual, group or an institution that has access to "power." The mistreatment may be emotional, verbal, mental, physical, economical, social and/or political.

People of Color

People of Color refers to people who are not Caucasian/white. The term "people of color" is preferable for several reasons. The word "minority" is becoming obsolete with the new demographics of the United States –in some states, the minority is fast becoming the majority. The term "minority" no longer refers to women, as women now comprise about 50% of the work force.

Prejudice

Prejudice is prejudging or making a decision about a person or group of people without sufficient knowledge. Prejudicial thinking is frequently based on stereotypes.

Racism

Racism is prejudice and/or discrimination based on the social construction of "race." Differences in biological characteristics (e.g., skin color, hair texture, eye shape) are used to support a system of inequities.

Scapegoating

Scapegoating is blaming an individual or group for something based on that person or group's identity when, in reality, the person or group is not responsible. Prejudicial thinking and discriminatory acts can lead to scapegoating.

Sexism

Sexism is prejudice and/or discrimination based on gender.

Sexual Orientation

The deep-seated direction of one's erotic, romantic, and affectional attraction to the same gender, to the opposite gender, or to both genders. People do not "choose" their sexual orientation; they discover their feelings of attraction. The only choice is whether or not to act on those feelings.

A Problem-Diagnosis Program

This program is designed to help you in diagnosing a problem that involves people working together in a group. In this program twelve separate steps are presented, each of which contains a complete and separate idea, question, or instruction. Be sure that you understand and complete each step before going on to the next one.

1. Identify the problem you wish to work on. Describe the problem as you now see it.

    _____

    _____

    _____

2. Most problem statements can be rephrased so that they describe two things:

    a. The situation as it is now.

    b. The situation as you would like it to be (the ideal).

    Restate your problem situation in these terms.

    _____

    _____

    _____

3. Most problem situations can be understood in terms of the forces that push toward improvement – in other words, helping forces and restraining forces. It is useful to analyze a problem by making lists of the helping and restraining forces affecting a situation. Think about these now and list them. Be sure to list as many as you can, not worrying at this point about how important each one is. Use additional paper if you need to.

Helping Forces	Restraining Forces

4. Review the two lists. Underline those forces that seem to be the most important right now, and that you think you might be able to influence constructively. Depending on the problem, there may be one specific force that stands out, or there may be two or three helping forces and two or three restraining forces that are particularly important.

5. Now, for each restraining force you have underlined, list some possible courses of action that you might be able to plan and carry out to reduce the effect of the force or to eliminate it completely. Brainstorm! List as many action steps as possible, without worrying about how effective or practical they would be. You will later have a chance to decide which are the most appropriate.

RESTRAINING FORCE A:

Possible action steps to reduce this force:

RESTRAINING FORCE B:

Possible action steps to reduce this force:

RESTRAINING FORCE C:

Possible action steps to reduce this force:

_____

_____

_____

6. Now do the same with each helping force you underlined. List all the action steps that come to mind that would increase the effect of each helping force.

HELPING FORCE A:

Possible action steps to increase this force:

_____

_____

_____

HELPING FORCE B:

Possible action steps to increase this force:

_____

_____

_____

HELPING FORCE C:

Possible action steps to increase this force:

_____

_____

_____

7. You have now listed possible action steps to change the key forces affecting your problem situation. Review these possible action steps and underline those that seem promising.

8. List the steps you have underlined. Then for each action step list the materials, people and other resources available to you to carrying out the action.

Action Steps	Resources Available

9. Review the list of action steps and resources and think about how each might fit into a comprehensive action plan. Take out those items that do not seem to fit into the overall plan, add any new steps and resources that will round out the plan, and think about a possible sequence of action.

_____

_____

_____

10. Plan a way of evaluating the effectiveness of your action program as it is implemented. Think about this now, and list the evaluation procedures you will use.

_____

_____

_____

11. You now have a plan of action to deal with the problem situation. The next step is for you to implement it.

GLOSSARY

Active Listening – A communication procedure in which the listener uses nonverbal behaviors, such as eye contact and gestures, as well as verbal behaviors, including tone of voice, open-ended questioning, restating, and summarizing, to demonstrate to the speaker that the listener is paying attention.

Avoidance – The practice of non-engagement.

Basic Needs – Needs that underlie all human behavior – survival, self-worth, belonging, self-actualization, power, freedom, fun…

Bias – A preconceived opinion or attitude about something or someone. A bias may be favorable or unfavorable.

Body Language – posture, body positions and looks while listening and speaking that reveal much information about how we feel and what we are thinking.

Brainstorming – sharing ideas that come to mind without judging whether they are good or bad.

Clarity – To make clearer or to enhance understanding. During a conflict-resolution procedure, open-ended questions are often used to clarify meaning.

Closed Questions – questions which can be answered with a simple response such as "yes", or "no" and which do not give us very much information.

Collaboration – Working with the other side to seek solutions that completely satisfy both parties. This involves accepting both parties' concerns as valid and digging into an issue in an attempt to find innovative possibilities. It also means being open and exploratory.

Common interests – Needs and/or interests that are identified as being held jointly by the parties in a conflict resolution process.

Competition – A strategy by which one pursues the satisfaction of one's own interests at the expense of others – a win-lose approach.

Compromise – An expedient settlement that only partially satisfies both sides. Compromising doesn't dig into the underlying problem, but rather seeks a more superficial arrangement such as "splitting the difference." It is based upon partial concessions – giving up something to get something.

Conflict – An expressed struggle between at least two interdependent parties who perceive incompatible goals, scarce resources, and interference from the other party in achieving their goals; a controversy or disagreement; to come into opposition.

Conflict Resolution – A spectrum of processes that utilize communication skills and creative thinking to develop voluntary solutions that are acceptable to those concerned in a dispute.

Cooperation – Associating for mutual benefit; working toward a common end of purpose.

Culture – That part of human interactions and experiences that determines how people feel, act, and think. It is through one's culture that one establishes standards to judge right from wrong, beauty and truth, and the worth of oneself and others. Culture includes one's nationality, ethnicity, race, gender, sexual orientation, socioeconomic background, ability, and age.

De-escalate – To engage in actions that decrease the intensity of a conflict.

Disputants – One who is engaged in a disagreement or conflict.

Escalate – To engage in particular actions that increase the intensity of a conflict.

Ground Rules – agreed upon standards of behavior that help make the mediation process.

"I" Statements – a way of expressing ourselves when we are using our "active listening" skills that takes responsibility for our feelings and expresses our needs. As mediators we try to help disputants use "I" statements in order to deescalate the conflict and promote healing communication.

Interest – A substantive, procedural, or psychological need of a party to a conflict; the aspect of something that makes it matter to someone.

Mediation – a process that allows people who are in conflict with each other to discuss things in a structured environment that facilitates a peaceful resolution that is fair to everyone.

Mediator – a person who is trained to help people resolve their disputes while remaining neutral.

Open Questions – questions that prompt the person being asked to offer more information which can help us understand how they are feeling or thinking.

Party – a side in the mediation (see disputant).

Position – A point of view; a specific solution that a party proposes to meet his or her interests or needs. A position is likely to be concrete or explicit, and it often includes a demand or threat that leaves little room for discussion. In conflict resolution, an essential activity is for participants to get beyond their positions to understanding their underlying interests and needs.

Resolve – To settle a conflict or disagreement through a process such as mediation.

Resolution – The actual details of the settlement or a conflict or disagreement.

Shared Interest – Something the parties can agree on or something they both want that can become the starting point of a possible agreement to the conflict.

Summarize – To restate in brief, concise form. Summarizing is an aspect of active listening that is utilized by both disputants and mediators to increase common understanding.

Trust – To have confidence in or to feel sure of, faith.

Value – A principle, standard or quality considered worthwhile or desirable.

Violence – The unjust or abusive use of power; force exerted for the purpose of injuring, damaging, or abusing people or property.